WISE INVESTING MADE SIMPLE

Larry Swedroe's Tales to Enrich Your Future

By
Larry E. Swedroe

Charter Financial Publishing Network
499 Broad Street
Shrewsbury, NJ 07702
Phone: 732-450-8866
Fax: 732-450-8877
www.fa-mag.com

Printed in the United States of America.
June 2007

Library of Congress Control Number: 2007929250
ISBN: 978-0-9766574-2-2

TABLE OF CONTENTS

If you tell me a fact, I learn; tell me a truth and I'll believe; but tell me a good story and it will live in my heart forever.

—Anonymous

Introduction

Most Americans, having taken a biology course in high school, know more about amoebas than they do about investing. Despite its obvious importance to every individual, our education system almost totally ignores the field of finance and investments. This is true unless you go to an undergraduate business school or pursue an M.B.A. in finance. For example, my daughter is a senior at the University of Illinois. She attended an excellent high school and graduated in the top 10 percent of her class. Having taken a biology course, she can tell you all you would ever need to know about amoebas. She could not, however, tell you the first thing about how financial markets work. She certainly could not tell you how markets set prices. Without that basic understanding, there is simply no way for her to know how to make investment decisions.

Most investors, many without realizing it, are in the same boat. They think they know how markets work, but the reality is quite different. As humorist Josh Billings noted: "It ain't what a man don't know as makes him a fool, but what he does know as ain't so." The result is that individuals are making investments without the basic knowledge required to understand the implications of their decisions. It is as if they took a trip to a place they have never been with neither a road map nor directions. Lacking a formal education in finance, most investors make decisions based upon the accepted conventional wisdom—ideas that have become so ingrained that few individuals question them.

Most of what you will read in this book directly contradicts the conventional wisdom that smart people, working diligently, can discover which stocks are mispriced by the market. Thus, they can buy stocks that are undervalued and avoid (or sell short) the stocks that are overvalued. This conventional wisdom also says these smart investors can also time the market—that is, they can get into the market before the bull enters the arena and sell before the bear emerges from its hibernation. This is what the practice of active management is all about—stock picking and market timing. Anything else is even considered by some to be un-American. To quote my ex-boss: "Diligence, hard work, research, and intelligence just have to pay off in superior results. How can no management be better than professional management?"

The problem with this thought process is that while these statements are correct generalizations (and as a result become conventional wisdom), *success* in beating the market is the exception to the rule. If hard work and diligence always produce superior results, how do you account for the failure of the majority of professional money managers (intelligent, capable, hard-working individuals) to beat the market year in and year out?

If you keep an open mind, you will find that when exposed to the light of logic and evidence you will be convinced that not only is the conventional wisdom wrong, but that it never made any sense in the first place. In fact, it is illogical. I am confident that you will find both the simple, yet compelling logic of the stories presented here, and the evidence supporting that logic, so overwhelming that you will be convinced of its accuracy. Remember, "The Earth is flat" was once conventional wisdom; as was "the Earth is the center of the universe." As these examples make clear, however, just because something is conventional wisdom doesn't make it correct. In other words, even if millions of people believe a foolish thing, it is still a foolish thing.

Legends do die hard—especially when there is an establishment (Wall Street and the financial media) that is interested in perpetuating the legend. Thus, this book has three objectives. The first is to explain how markets really work, doing so in a way that makes it easy to understand even difficult concepts. I hope to accomplish this objective through the use of stories and analogies that present the logic in a paradigm with which you are already familiar, and then relate that logic to the world of investing. If you understand the logic in the story it should be just as clear when the logic is related to investing—especially when the evidence supports the logic.

If I am successful in meeting the first objective, I will have also achieved the second objective—to forever change the way you think about investing and how markets work.

The third objective is to provide you with sufficient knowledge to begin to make more informed and more prudent investment decisions.

The book was written with two audiences in mind. The first is individual investors. The second is financial advisors. Hopefully, my stories will provide advisors with the ammunition they need to convince their clients to stop throwing their hard earned money away, to stop making brokers and fund families wealthy, and to start playing the winner's game.

The winning strategy is actually simple and takes less energy. Thus, the strategy is not only likely to dramatically increase the odds of achieving your financial goals, but it will also allow you to improve the quality of your life, as the tale of The Big Rocks (chapter 23) illustrates. The way smart money invests today is by building a globally diversified portfolio of passively managed funds (i.e., index funds [including exchange-traded funds] and passive asset class funds) and staying the course, ignoring the noise of the market and the investment propaganda put out by Wall Street and the financial media.

One of my favorite expressions is "If you think education is expensive, try ignorance." Hopefully this book will whet your appetite for a deeper understanding of the issues raised and create a desire to broaden your knowledge. If you find this book both entertaining and educational, I have authored four other books on investing, *The Only Guide to a Winning Investment Strategy You'll Ever Need, What Wall Street Doesn't Want You To Know, Rational Investing In Irrational Times*, and *The Successful Investor Today: 14 Simple Truths You Must Know When You Invest*. In addition, I have co-authored, along with my partner Joe Hempen, a fifth book, *The Only Guide to a Winning Bond Strategy You'll Ever Need*. Each of the books goes into greater depth than the scope of this book allowed, and they also cover many important topics not covered here.

Note that I have included a few classic stories because their sage messages about investing and life are not to be missed.

I do not believe that they [investment advisors] can identify, in advance, the top-performing managers—no one can—and, I'd avoid those who claim they can do so.

—John Bogle

Chapter 1:
The Names Are Never the Same

Paula had just inherited $5 million dollars. She was quite concerned about how she was going to manage this large sum of money, especially since she recognized that she knew little about investing. She contacted her attorney and asked him for some advice.

The attorney gave Paula the names of two investment advisors that he recommended she interview. One was an advisor that worked for a local accounting firm that had established an affiliated registered investment advisor firm. The other was a broker who worked for Morgan Stanley.

Paula knew and trusted one of the partners at the CPA firm that was also an investment advisor. So she decided to first meet with that firm. When she called to set up an appointment, the advisor told her that he was going to send her a copy of the book, *The Only Guide to a Winning Investment Strategy You'll Ever Need*. He explained that the book provided an explanation of the firm's investment philosophy in simple terms. He also explained that the firm's philosophy was based on findings from academic research. He hoped that she would read the book prior to the meeting, as that would make the meeting more productive. She agreed to read the book in preparation for the meeting.

At the meeting the advisor explained that at the core of the firm's philosophy was the belief that it was difficult to beat the market, and that while a small percentage of money managers did so, no one had found a way to identify them *ahead of time*. Thus, the firm's belief was that the most important investment decision was not which manager to hire. Instead, the firm focused on the asset allocation decision—how much should be invested in risky stocks versus safer bonds. Thus, the first task would be to work with her to determine just how much risk she had the ability, willingness and need to take. He then explained that since there was no way to determine ahead of time which managers would be among the few that would outperform, the prudent approach was to accept market returns by investing in index funds and their similar, but more sophisticated, versions known as passive asset class funds. He then showed her the results of a study that demonstrated that over the long term 80 percent of pension plans that had tried to beat the market had failed to do so.

Paula left feeling comfortable with the approach of the advisor. The next day she met with the broker from Morgan Stanley. The broker explained that their investment approach was to hire the best investment managers in the world. They had a team of people that performed extensive due diligence so that they could find the best of the best. He asked Paula, "Isn't that who you want to manage your money?"

Paula recalled her conversation with the advisor. She asked the broker what he thought of indexing as a strategy. The broker responded: "Indexing is a perfectly good strategy—if you are willing to accept average returns. Our clients want to do better than that. We help them achieve that objective. You don't want to be average, do you Paula?"

The broker then showed Paula a list of the funds that the firm was currently recommending. He also showed her the performance history of the funds. To Paula's surprise, the firm's list had indeed outperformed similar index funds. This conflicted with what the other advisor had said. The broker had presented a compelling case. And Morgan Stanley was a prestigious firm. Surely she could trust them.

Paula was now confused. She did not know which way to turn, or who to believe. One of the two advisors was wrong. She decided to call the partner at the CPA firm and set up another meeting with their advisor. The advisor was pleased to meet with her and said he would be happy to answer any questions.

Paula brought the broker's list of fund recommendations to the meeting. She said, "I am confused. You told me that no one had found a way to identify which funds would outperform the market. When I met with the broker from Morgan Stanley he showed me this list of funds they were buying for their clients and they had outperformed the market over the past five years. How do you explain that?"

The advisor responded: "Paula, I am glad you asked that question. It is the question I am most often asked. You see it is easy to identify which funds have outperformed the market in the *past*. Any one with access to a database can do that. The question, however, is not whether you can identify which funds *have* outperformed the market. Instead, the question is can you identify them *ahead of time!*"

The advisor suggested that Paula set up another meeting with the stockbroker and ask him two questions. He said, "First, ask him to provide you with the list of funds his firm was recommending five years ago. If the names don't match then you have to ask the question why not? If the list had predictive ability would not the fund names be the same on both lists? If the names are not the same, something must have gone wrong. If something went wrong last time, can you confidently expect that something similar will not happen with your money? I can tell you that we have suggested this to many people and the client almost never gets to see the old list. You can guess why. And in the few cases that they do get to see the old list, the names are almost never the same."

Then the advisor played for Paula an excerpt of an interview between John Stossel and a well-known Wall Street advisor, Robert Stovall. The interview took place on November 27, 1992 on the popular television show "20/20." Stossel asked Stovall about the persistently poor performance of mutual fund managers. Stovall responded: "One-third of the money managers tend to beat the market every year." Stossel replied: "Two-thirds do worse!" Stovall responded: "But it's different ones each time."

Paula had to laugh. Was this guy serious? If it is a different group every year how was she, or anyone else, going to be able to identify the ones that will outperform in the future? Paula then asked the advisor, "What is the other question you would like me to ask?"

The advisor responded: "Paula, we would never advise a client to invest in something we would not invest in ourselves. All of the partners in our firm, including me, invest their assets in the same funds we advise our clients to invest in. Of course the percentage that is invested in each fund is different for everyone because it is tailored to each person's unique situation. In addition, our profit sharing plan is invested in the same funds. I would be more than happy to show you my brokerage statement so that you can see that this is true."

Paula told him that it would not be necessary. The advisor continued: "Ask the broker to show you his financial statement and see the funds in which he has invested. Then ask him to show you the list of funds that are available inside of Morgan Stanley's 401(k) plan. If the funds on both lists are not the same as the names on the list of recommended funds, what does that tell you?"

Paula was impressed with the advisor. Everything he said seemed like common sense to her. And he was able to back up every statement with facts, not hype. She thanked him for his time and promised she would return to the broker, ask those questions, and let him know her decision.

Paula set up another meeting with the broker. She asked him to provide the list of recommended funds from five years ago. The broker stared at her with the look of a deer caught in a car's headlights. He had gone through Morgan Stanley's intensive sales program. The training program had taught him to ask questions like "You don't want to be average do you?" But it had not prepared him for this question. He was taught to sell, and obfuscate, but not to answer questions like this. He told Paula that he would have to dig that information up as no one had ever asked him that before. She then asked him to also provide her with a list of both his own investments as well as a list of the funds available within the firm's 401(k) plan. The broker told her he would have to get back to her.

Paula was not surprised that she never heard back from the broker. She called the partner at the CPA firm and told him that she had decided to use the firm's advisory services. The partner told her that he was confident that she would not regret the decision. Paula was confident that he was right.

The Moral of the Tale

The moral of this tale is that before you trust your assets to an investment advisor, ask the questions that Paula asked the broker.

The next story is the most important one in the book, as it explains how the market prices of securities are established. Understanding this is critical to determining a winning investment strategy.

It is not easy to get rich in Las Vegas, at Churchill Downs, or at the local Merrill Lynch office.

—Paul Samuelson

Chapter 2:
How Markets Set Prices

On any given Saturday during the college basketball season there may be one hundred games being played. In some of those games it is easy to identify the better team. For example, Duke is a perennial contender for the national college basketball championship. Their illustrious coach, Mike Krzyzewski (Coach K), is a graduate of West Point. Each year he schedules a game with Army as a favor to his alma mater. Though the likelihood of Army winning is about as likely as the sun rising in the west, the game does generate a large amount of revenue for West Point. These types of mismatches are known as "cupcake" games.

Every major school has a few cupcake games on their schedule, particularly early in the season. Even a fan with limited knowledge would be able to predict the winner of this type of game the majority of the time. A fan that was an "expert" would be able to predict the winner at least 90 percent of the time. The reason is simple. Duke has better shooters, better rebounders, better defenders, quicker athletes that can also jump higher, a better coach, better training facilities, and so on. This makes it easy to identify which team will likely win a game between Army and Duke.

On the other hand, there are many games in which it is more difficult to predict the winner. This is especially true later in the season when conference play begins. A good example of a game that is typically difficult to predict the winner of would be when the Duke Blue Devils plays their hated rival the Tar Heels of North Carolina. Since a monkey throwing darts would be expected to predict the winner of such games 50 percent of the time, a fan with limited knowledge should be expected to do no worse. A fan with "expert" knowledge should, however, be able to do better than monkeys. Perhaps such an expert might be able to forecast the winner of these types of games with an accuracy of 60 percent.

Most of us know at least a few individuals who think they are experts on sports. Some may even have an account with a local bookie or a Las Vegas book-making firm. As we said earlier, such experts are likely to be able to predict the winners of the cupcake games with 90 percent accuracy, and the winners of the remainder of the games with an accuracy of 60 percent. Thus,, they might be expected to be able to predict the winner of all games with an accuracy of perhaps 75 percent. But the story gets even better—these experts don't have to bet on all the games. They can avoid betting on the games when it is difficult to predict the winner. They can limit the selection of games on which they place a bet to only those games where they are highly confident they can predict the winner. By so doing they can be confident that they will be successful at least 90 percent of the time. Yet despite the ability to bet only on games where there is a greater than 90 percent chance of being able to predict the winner correctly, it is unlikely that you know even a single person that has become rich betting on sporting events. It is also likely that you don't know anyone that knows anyone that has made his fortune in that way. On the other hand, you might know someone that has made a small fortune betting on sporting events by starting out with a large one!

With the odds of success of being able to predict winners so high, why don't we know people who have achieved great wealth by betting on sports? The answer is quite simple—you cannot simply bet on Duke to beat Army. If you want to bet on Duke to beat Army you might have to provide the counter-party to your bet with a handicap (known as the *point spread*) of perhaps forty points. In other words, Duke not only has to beat Army, they have to beat them by more than forty points for you to win the bet. This *point spread* is the reason we don't hear about rich gamblers, only rich bookies. And the reason we hear about rich bookies is that gambling involves costs. Consider the following example.

Mark is a Duke fan and bets on the Blue Devils to beat Army by more than forty points. In betting lingo Mark "gives" points. Steve is a graduate of West Point and even though he knows Duke is likely to beat Army he doesn't think it likely that they will do so by such a large margin. Thus, he "takes" the points and bets on Army. If Mark and Steve are friends and they bet against each other we have what is known as a zero-sum game. For example, if they bet $10, one would win $10 and the other would lose $10. The net of the two is zero. On the other hand, if they made a bet through a bookie, each would have to bet $11 to win just $10. This becomes a negative sum game for Mark and Steve. The winner of the bet will win $10. The loser, however, is out $11. The difference of $1 is known as the "vigorish." It is a profit for the bookie. The game for Mark and Steve has become a negative sum. Note that the bookies win whether you win or lose. They just need you to play in order for them to win. I hope you are beginning to see the analogy to investing—we could compare a stockbroker to a bookie! They win whether you win or lose. They only need you to play for them to win. Perhaps that is why Woody Allen said "A stockbroker is someone who invests your money until it is all gone." One translation: The objective of a stockbroker is to transfer assets from your account to their account. As my good friend, and author of three wonderful books, Bill Bernstein says: "The stockbroker services his clients in the same way that Bonnie and Clyde serviced banks."[1]

Continuing our story, it is important to understand who sets the point spreads. Most people believe that it is the bookies that determine the spread. Although that is the conventional wisdom, it is incorrect. It is the market that determines the point spread. The bookies only set the *initial* spread. This is an important point to understand. Let's begin with an understanding of whether the bookies want to *make* bets or *take* bets—and there is a difference between the two.

If the bookies were to make bets, they might actually lose money by being on the wrong side of the bet. Again, think of a stockbroker. If you want to buy a stock (making a bet on the company), you have to buy it from someone. A stockbroker is not going to sell that stock to you because he might lose money. Instead, he finds someone that wants to sell the stock and matches the buyer with the seller. He is *taking* bets, not *making* bets. In the process he earns the vigorish (a commission). Like stockbrokers, bookies want to *take* bets, not *make* them. Thus, they set the initial point spread at the "price" they believe will balance the forces of supply and demand (the point at which an equal amount of money will be bet on Duke and Army). To illustrate how the process works, consider the following example.

What would happen if a bookie made a terrible mistake and posted a point spread of zero in the Duke versus Army game? Obviously, gamblers would rush to bet on Duke. The result would be an imbalance of supply and demand. The bookies would end up making bets—something they are loath to do.

Like with any market, an excess of demand leads to an increase in price. The point spread would begin to rise, and it would continue to rise until supply equals demand, and the bookies had an equal amount of money bet on both sides (or at least as close to that as they could manage). At that point they are taking bets, not making them. And the bookies would win no matter the outcome of the game.

In one of my favorite films, *Trading Places*, Eddie Murphy makes a similar observation about the commodity brokerage firm of Duke and Duke. When the Duke brothers explain that they get a commission on every trade, whether the clients make money or not, Murphy exclaims: "Well it sounds to me like you guys are a couple of bookies."

As you can see, it is the market that determines the point spread (or the price of Duke). In other words, it is a bunch of amateurs like you and me (and

I played college basketball), who think they know something about sports, that are setting the spread. And even with a bunch of amateurs setting the spread (not the professional bookies) most of us don't know anyone that has become rich betting on sports. It seems that a bunch of amateurs are setting point spreads at prices that make it extremely difficult for even the most knowledgeable sports fan to exploit any mispricing, after accounting for the expenses of the effort. The important term here is *after expenses.*

Because of the vigorish, it is not enough to be able to win more than 50 percent of the bets. With a vigorish of 10 percent, a bettor (investor) would have to be correct about 53 percent of the time to come out ahead. And that assumes there are no other costs involved (including the value of the time it takes to study the teams, analyze the spread and make the bet).

In economic terms, a market in which it is difficult to persistently exploit mispricings after the expenses of the effort is called an *efficient market.* Because we don't know of people that have become rich betting on sports, we know intuitively that sports betting markets are efficient. However, intuition is often incorrect. It helps to have evidence supporting your intuition. Before we look at the evidence, however, we need a definition.

Point Spreads and Random Errors

An *unbiased estimator* is a statistic that is on average neither too high nor too low. The method of estimation does not always produce estimates that correspond to reality, but errors in either direction are equally likely. It turns out that the point spread is an unbiased estimate of the outcome of sporting events—while it is not expected to be correct in every instance, when it is incorrect the errors are randomly distributed with a zero mean. To make this clear, we return to our Duke versus Army example in which Duke was favored by forty points. Duke does not have to win by *exactly* forty points for the market in sports betting to be considered efficient. In fact, the likelihood of Duke winning by exactly that amount would be very low. However, that is not relevant to the issue of whether or not the market for sports betting is efficient. What is relevant is whether you can predict whether Duke will win by more than forty or less than forty. If half the time they win by more, and half the time they win by less, and there is no way to know when they will be above or below the point spread, the point spread is an unbiased predictor—and the market is efficient. With this understanding we are ready to examine the evidence.

Examining the Evidence

Research has found that point spreads are accurate in the sense that they are *unbiased predictors.* For example, in a study covering six NBA seasons, Raymond Sauer found that the average difference between point spreads and actual point differences was less than one-quarter of one point.[2] When you consider that, on average, the market guessed the actual resulting point spread with an error of less than one-quarter of one point, and there is a 10 percent cost of playing, it is easy to understand why we don't know people that have become rich from betting on sports. And it is easy to see that the market in sports betting is what economists call efficient. The important lesson is that while it is often easy to identify the better team (in this case Duke) that is not a *sufficient* condition for exploiting the market. It is only a *necessary* condition. The *sufficient* condition is that you have to be able to exploit any mispricing by the market. For example, if you knew that Duke should be favored by forty points, but the point spread was only thirty points, and you could consistently identify such opportunities, then the market would be inefficient. This, however, is not the case.

Horse racing presents an even more amazing outcome, especially when you consider the following. My mother loved to go to the track. Like many people she chose the horses on which she would bet by either the color of the jockey's outfit or the name of the horse. If the jockey wore purple, forget about it. She hated the color purple. And she always bet on the three horse in the first race. Now there are fans that go to the track and make a "science" of studying each horse's racing history and under what racing conditions the horse did well or poorly. And perhaps these experts even attend workouts to time the horses. So we have these "experts" competing against people like my mother. Yet, the final odds, which reflects the judgment of all bettors, reliably predict the outcome—the favorite wins the most often, the second favorite is the next most likely to win, and so on. It gets even better in that a horse with three-to-one odds wins about one-fourth of the time![3] It seems that the collective wisdom of the crowd is a tough competitor indeed.

An Efficient Market

An efficient market is one in which trading systems fail to produce excess returns because everything *currently* knowable is already incorporated into prices (Duke is so much better than Army they should be favored by forty points, but not more). The next piece of available information will be random as to whether it will be better or worse than the market already expects. The only way to beat an efficient market is to either know something that the market doesn't know—such as the fact that a team's best player is injured and will not be able to play—or to be able to interpret information about the teams better than the market (other gamblers collectively) does. You have to search for a game where the strength of the favorite is underestimated or the weakness of the underdog overestimated; and thus the spread, or the market, is wrong. The spread is really the competition. And the spread is determined by the collective wisdom of the entire market. This is an important point to understand. Let's see why.

Returning to our example of Mark and Steve betting on Duke versus Army, if there was no sports betting market to which Mark and Steve could refer they would have to set the point spread themselves—instead of the market setting the spread. Now Mark might be a more knowledgeable fan than Steve, who also happens to be a graduate of West Point. Steve's heart might also influence his thinking. Thus, when Mark offers to give Steve thirty points, Steve jumps at the chance and bets on Army. Mark has just exploited Steve's lack of knowledge. (Mark might still lose the bet, but the odds of winning the bet have increased in his favor.)

The existence of an efficient public market in which the knowledge of all investors is at work in setting prices serves to protect the less informed bettors (investors) from being exploited. The flip side is that the existence of an efficient market prevents the sophisticated and more knowledgeable bettors (investors) from exploiting their less knowledgeable counterparts. And, as we have seen, the spread is an unbiased predictor and the market is efficient. The result is that the *market* is a tough competitor.

There are other important points to understand about sports betting and how it relates to investing. The first is that in the world of sports betting it is a bunch of amateurs that are setting prices. Even though that is the case, we saw that it is difficult to find pricing errors that could be exploited. In the world of investing, however, it is professionals that are setting prices.

It is estimated that about 80 percent of all trading is done by large institutional traders. In fact, the most active fifty institutions account for about one-half of all trading on the New York Stock Exchange.[4] Thus, they are the ones setting prices, not amateur individual investors. With professionals (instead of amateurs) dominating the market, the competition is certainly tougher. Every time an individual buys a stock he should consider that he is competing with these giant institutional investors. The individual investor should also acknowledge that it is the institutions that have more resources, and thus it is more likely that they will succeed.

Another difference between sports betting and investing is best illustrated by returning to our example of Duke versus Army. Imagine that you are best friends with Coach K. As a birthday present he invites you into the Duke locker room to meet the players and hear the pregame talk. As the players are exiting the locker room to start warming up, Duke's star point guard trips over a water bucket and breaks his ankle. Your mercenary instincts take over and you immediately pull out your cell phone and place a large bet on Army, taking forty points. You possessed information that others did not have and took advantage of it. And the best part is that there is nothing illegal about that "trade." Now remember that it is likely that few, if any, of us knows anyone that has become rich betting on sports, despite the existence of rules that allow you to exploit what in the world of investing would be considered inside information. And in the world of investing it is illegal to trade and profit from inside information, as Martha Stewart found out. Even individuals who have had inside information, such as Pete Rose, and could influence the outcomes of sporting events, don't seem to be able to persistently exploit such information.

The conclusion that we can draw from the evidence is that the markets for betting on sports are highly efficient. This is true despite both the lack of rules against insider trading and the fact that it is a bunch of amateurs that *think they know* something about sports (and often bet on their home team or alma mater with their hearts and not their heads) that are setting prices. In the world of investing there are specific rules against insider trading and the competition is tougher since it is the professional investors who are setting prices. In addition, as is the case with sports betting, being smarter than the market is not enough because there are costs involved. In sports betting, the cost is the vigorish. The problem for those investors trying to exploit mispricings in the stock market is that there are also costs involved. Like with sports betting, the "bookies" (brokerage firms) have to be paid when active investors place their bets. Trading involves not only commissions, but also the spread between the bid (the price dealers are willing to pay) and the offer (the price at which dealers are willing to sell). If you place your assets with a mutual fund, you also have to pay the operating costs of the mutual fund—which are generally higher for actively managed funds than for passively managed ones. And for institutional investors costs may also include what are called market-impact costs as well. Market impact is what occurs when a mutual fund (or other investor) wants to buy or sell a large block of stock. The fund's purchases or sales will cause the stock to move beyond its current bid (lower) or offer (higher) price, increasing the cost of trading. For taxable accounts, there is also the burden of capital gains taxes that is created by actively trading the portfolio.

We continue with our analogy between sports betting and investing by examining how investors set the prices of individual stocks.

How Stock Prices Are Set

Stock prices are set in a similar manner to how point spreads are established. A good analogy to the point spread setting process is how underwriters set the price of an *initial public offering* (IPO). Just as bookies survey the market to set the initial point spread so that supply will equal demand (so that they can take bets, not make them), underwriters survey potential investors and set the price based on their best estimate of the price needed to sell all the shares. Once the IPO is completed the shares will trade in what is called the secondary market. Just as with sports betting, in the secondary market the forces of supply and demand take over. The only difference is that instead of point spreads setting prices, they are determined by the price-to-earnings (P/E) ratio or the book-to-market (BtM) ratio. The P/E and BtM ratios act just like the point spread. The following example will make this clear.

Battle of the Discount Stores

As an investor you are faced with the decision to purchase the shares of either Wal-Mart or JC Penney. Wal-Mart is generally considered to be one of the top retailers. It has great management, the best store locations, an outstanding inventory management system, a strong balance sheet, etc. Because of its great prospects, Wal-Mart is considered a growth stock. JC Penney, on the other hand, is a weak company. It has had poor management, old stores in bad locations, a balance sheet that has been devastated by weak earnings, etc. JC Penney is a company that is distressed. Because of its poor prospects, JC Penney is considered a value stock. Just as it was easy to identify the better team in the Duke versus Army example, it is easy to identify the better company when faced with choosing between Wal-Mart and JC Penney. Most individuals faced with having to buy either Wal-Mart or JC Penney would not even have to think about the decision—they would rush to buy Wal-Mart. But is that the right choice?

As we saw in the sports betting story, being able to identify the better team did not help us make the decision as to which one was the better bet. Let's see if the ability to identify the better company helps us make an investment decision. Before reading on, think about which company is Duke and which one is Army.

Imagine that both Wal-Mart and JC Penney have earnings of $1 per share. That is certainly possible even though Wal-Mart generates far more profits. Wal-Mart might have one billion shares outstanding and JC Penney might only have one hundred million shares outstanding. Now imagine a world where Wal-Mart and JC Penney both traded at a price of 10. Which stock would you buy in that world? Clearly you would rush to buy Wal-Mart. The problem is that Wal-Mart is Duke and JC Penney is Army. And Wal-Mart and JC Penney trading at the same price is analogous to the point spread in the Duke versus Army game being set by the bookies at zero. Hell will freeze over before either happens. Just as sports fans would rush in and bet on Duke, driving up the point spread until the odds of winning the bet were equal, investors would drive up the price of Wal-Mart relative to the price of JC Penney until the *risk-adjusted expected* returns from investing in either stock were equal. Let's see how that might look in terms of prices for the shares of Wal-Mart and JC Penney.

Being a weak company, with relatively poor prospects, investors might be willing to pay just seven times earnings for the stock of JC Penney. Thus, with earnings of $1 per share the stock would trade at $7. The company might also have a book value of $7 per share. Thus, the BtM would be 1 ($7 book value divided by its $7 market price). On the other hand, Wal-Mart is not only a safer investment due to its stronger balance sheet, but it has outstanding growth prospects. Thus, investors might be willing to pay thirty times earnings for Wal-Mart stock. Thus, with $1 per share in earnings, the stock would trade at $30. The company might also have a book value of just $3 per share. Thus, the BtM would be 0.1 ($3 book value divided by its $30 market price). Wal-Mart is trading at a P/E ratio that is over four times that of the P/E ratio of JC Penney. It is also trading at a BtM that is only one-tenth that of the BtM of JC Penney. Wal-Mart is Duke having to give Army forty points to make Army an equally good bet.

The Financial Equivalent of the Point Spread

The P/E and the BtM ratios act just like point spreads. The only difference is that instead of having to give away a lot of points to bet on a great team to win, you have to pay a higher price relative to earnings and book value for a great glamour company than for a distressed value company. If you bet on the underdog (Army) you get the point spread in your favor. Similarly, if you invest in a distressed value company (JC Penney) you pay a low price relative to earnings and book value. The great sports team (Duke) has to overcome large point spreads to win the bet. The great company (Wal-Mart) has to overcome the high price you pay in order to produce above market returns. In gambling the middlemen who always win as long as you play are the bookies. In investing, the middlemen who always win—as long as you try to pick mutual funds or stocks that will outperform—are the active fund managers and the stockbrokers. They win regardless of whether you win or not. They win as long as you agree to play—betting that one fund, or one stock, is going to out-perform another.

Let's again consider the analogy between sports betting and investing in stocks. First, in sports betting sometimes it is easy to identify the better team (Duke versus Army) and sometimes it is more difficult (Duke versus North Carolina). The same is true of stocks. It is easy to identify which company, Wal-Mart or JC Penney, is the superior one. On the other hand, it is harder when our choices are Wal-Mart and Costco.

Second, in sports betting we don't have to bet on all the games, we can choose to bet only on the games in which we can easily identify the better team. Similarly we don't have to invest in all stocks. We can choose to invest only in the stocks of the superior companies.

Third, in sports the problem with betting on the good teams is that the rest of the market also knows that they are superior and you have to give away lots of points. The point spread eliminates any advantage gained by betting on the superior team. The same is true with investing. The price you have to pay for investing in superior companies is a higher P/E ratio (offsetting the more rapid growth in earnings that are expected) and a lower BtM (offsetting the lesser risk of the greater company). In sports, the pricing mechanism in place would make betting on either team an equally good bet. The same applies for invest-ing: Either stock would make an equally good investment. Thus,, while being able to identify the better team (company) is a *necessary* condition of success, it is not a *sufficient* one.

Fourth, when a bet is placed between friends it is a zero-sum game. However, when the bet is placed with a bookie the game becomes a negative-sum one because of the costs involved (the bookies win). Since we cannot trade stocks between friends, trading stocks must be a negative-sum game because of the costs involved (the market makers earn the bid-offer spread, the stockbrokers charge commissions, the active managers charge large fees, and Uncle Sam collects taxes).

Fifth, in the world of sports betting it should be relatively easy to exploit mispricing because it is amateurs that are the competition setting prices. In the world of investing the competition is tougher since the competition is mostly large institutional investors, not amateurs like you and me.

Sixth, in sports betting it is legal to trade on inside information. Yet even with such an advantage it is likely that you don't know anyone who has become rich by exploiting this type of knowledge. On the other hand, it is ille-gal to trade on inside information regarding stocks. Thus, it must be even more difficult to win that game.

The evidence from the world of investing supports the logic of the above arguments. Study after study demonstrates that the majority of both individual and institutional investors who attempt to beat the market by either picking stocks or timing the market fail miserably, and do so with great persistence. The following is a brief summary of the evidence.

Individual Investors
University of California professors Brad Barber and Terrance Odean have produced a series of landmark studies on the performance of individual investors. One study found that the stocks individual investors buy underperform the market after they buy them, and the stocks they sell outperform after they sell them.[5] They also found that male investors underperform the market by about 3 percent per annum and women (because they trade less and thus incur less costs) trail the market by about 2 percent per annum.[6] In addition, they found that those investors who traded the most trailed the market on a risk-adjusted basis by over 10 percent per annum.[7] And to prove that more heads are not better than one, they found that investment clubs trailed the market by almost 4 percent per annum.[8] Since all the above figures are on a pretax basis, once taxes are taken into account the story would become even more dismal. Perhaps it was this evidence that convinced Andrew Tobias, author of *The Only Investment Book You Will Ever Need*, to offer this sage advice: "If you find yourself tempted to ask the question what stock should I buy, resist the temptation. If you do ask, don't listen. And if you hear an answer, promise yourself that you will ignore it."[9]

Institutional Investors
Institutional investors don't fare much better than individual investors. Mark Carhart's study, "On Persistence in Mutual Funds," analyzed 1,892 mutual funds for the period 1962-93. Based on the conclusions reached in this landmark study, once one accounts for common risk factors such as size and value, the average equity fund underperformed its appropriate style benchmark by about 1.8 percent per annum on a pretax basis.

Carhart, currently the co-head of the quantitative strategies group at Goldman Sachs, also found no evidence of any persistence in outperformance beyond the randomly expected.[10] And if there is no persistence in performance, there is no way to identify the few future winners ahead of time. The figures here are all on a pretax basis as well. Thus, the effect of taxes on after-tax returns would make the story even worse.

The Moral of the Tale

All good stories have morals. So what is the moral of this tale? The moral is that betting against an efficient market is a loser's game. It doesn't matter whether the "game" is betting on a sporting event or trying to identify which stocks are going to outperform the market. While it is possible to win betting on sporting events, because the markets are highly efficient the only likely winners are the bookies. In addition, the more you play the game, the more likely it is you will lose and the bookies will win. The same is true of investing. And the reason is that the securities markets are also highly efficient.

If you are trying to time the market or pick stocks, you are playing a loser's game. Just as it is possible that by betting on sporting events you can win, it is possible that by picking stocks, timing the market, or using active managers to play the game on your behalf you will win (outperform). However, the odds of winning are poor. And just as with gambling, the more and the longer you play the game, the more likely it is that you will lose (as the costs of playing compound). This makes accepting market returns (passive investing) the winner's game.

By investing in passively managed funds and adopting a simple buy, hold, and rebalance strategy, you are guaranteed to not only earn market rates of returns, but you will do so in a low-cost and relatively tax-efficient manner. You are also virtually guaranteed to outperform the majority of professional and individual investors. Thus, it is the strategy most likely to achieve the best results. The bottom line is that while gamblers make bets (speculate on individual stocks and actively managed funds), investors let the markets work for them, not against them.

This quote sums up this tale: "Information isn't in the hands of one person. It's dispersed across many people. So relying on only your private information to make a decision guarantees that it will be less informed than it could be."[11]

Epilogue

Sometimes bookies lose their way and forget the winning strategy. Trouble begins when bookies are unable to "lay off" bets—make sure that an equal amount of money is bet on Duke and Army. Thus, they end up making bets instead of taking them. And as we have seen, that is the loser's game. Consider the example of one bookie, the owner of the on-line casino Aces Gold Casino.

The bookie had lost some money when he could not maintain a balanced book and ended up on the wrong side of the bet. Instead of trying to catch up gradually, he abandoned the winning strategy of only taking bets, not making them. He began to tilt his point spreads (relative to other bookmakers) to one team. This ensured that he would attract a lot of bets on one team and little to none on the other. Unfortunately, he kept losing. By the time of the 2002 NFL Super Bowl, the most heavily wagered sporting event, he owed his clients more than a million dollars. So he went for the proverbial "Hail Mary." Prior to the game, the standard line favored the St. Louis Rams over the New England Patriots by fourteen points. In order to attract a large amount of bets, Aces Gold offered those betting on the Patriots an extra one-half point, placing the spread at fourteen and one-half points. Predictably, Aces Gold Casino took in a large amount of bets on the Patriots—and made no effort to "lay off" those bets.

"Not only did the Rams not cover the spread, but they also lost the game in a stunning upset. Aces Gold owed gamblers more than $3 million, money that they would never see. The bookie is now rumored to be living somewhere in Texas."[12] Or, perhaps he is wearing "cement shoes."

The next story also relates to market efficiency and choosing the winning strategy.

The most common of all follies is to believe passionately in the palpably not true.

—H. L. Mencken

Chapter 3:
The Twenty-Dollar Bill

There is an old story about a financial economist who also happened to be a passionate defender of the efficient markets hypothesis (EMH). He was walking down the street with a friend. The friend stops and says: "Look there is a $20 bill on the ground." The economist turns and says: "Can't be. If there was a $20 bill on the ground somebody would have already picked it up." This joke is told by those that believe that the markets are inefficient and that investors can thus outperform the market by exploiting mispricings—finding an undervalued stock instead of a $20 bill. It is actually a misleading analogy to the EMH. The following version is a much better one.

A financial economist, and passionate defender of the EMH, was walking down the street with a friend. The friend stops and says: "Look there is a $20 bill on the ground." The economist turns and says: "Boy, this must be our lucky day! Better pick that up quick because the market is so efficient it won't be there for long. Finding a $20 bill lying around happens so infrequently that it would be foolish to spend our time searching for more of them. Certainly, after assigning a value to the time spent in the effort, an 'investment' in trying to find money lying on the street just waiting to be picked up would be a poor one. I am certainly not aware of any one who has achieved their wealth by 'mining' beaches with metal detectors." When he had finished they both looked down and the $20 bill was gone!

There is also what might be called "The Hollywood Version" of this story. A financial economist, and passionate defender of the EMH, was walking down the street with a friend. The friend stops and says: "Look there is a $20 bill on the ground." The economist turns and says: "Can't be. If there was a $20 bill on the ground somebody would have already picked it up." The friend bends down and picks up the $20 bill and dashes off. He then decides that this is an easy way to make a living. He abandons his job and begins to search the world for $20 bills lying on the ground waiting to be picked up. A year later the economist is walking down the same street and sees his long lost friend lying on the sidewalk wearing torn and filthy clothing. Appalled to see the disheveled state into which his friend had sunk, he rushes over to find out what had happened. The friend tells that him that he never again found another $20 bill lying on the ground.

Those that tell the first version of the story fail to understand that an efficient market doesn't mean that there cannot be a $20 bill lying around. Instead, it means that it is so unlikely that you will find one that it does not pay to go looking for them—the costs of the effort are likely to exceed the benefits. In addition, if it became known that there were lots of $20 bills to be found in a certain area everyone would be there competing to find them. That reduces the likelihood of achieving an appropriate "return on investment."

The analogy to the EMH is that it is not impossible to uncover an anomaly (that $20 bill lying on the floor) that can be exploited (being able to buy a stock that is somehow undervalued by the market). Instead, one of the fundamental tenets of the EMH is that in a competitive financial environment successful trading strategies self-destruct because they are self-limiting—when they are discovered they are eliminated by the very act of exploiting the strategy. Economics professors Dwight Lee and James Verbrugge of the University of Georgia explained the power of the efficient markets theory in the following manner:

> "The efficient market theory is practically alone among theories in that it becomes more powerful when people discover serious inconsistencies between it and the real world. If a clear efficient market anomaly is discovered, the behavior (or lack of behavior) that gives rise to it will tend to be eliminated by competition among investors for higher returns. [For example] If stock prices are found to follow predictable seasonal patterns unrelated to financially relevant considerations, this knowledge will elicit responses that have the effect of eliminating the very patterns they were designed to exploit. The implication here is rather striking. The more empirical flaws that are discovered in the efficient market theory, the more robust the theory becomes. [In effect] Those who do the most to ensure that the efficient market theory remains fundamental to our understanding of financial economics are not its intellectual defenders, but those mounting the most serious empirical assault against it."[1]

The "January Effect"

The following example demonstrates how the efficiency of markets rapidly eliminates opportunities for abnormal profits. Imagine that an investor discovered that small-cap stocks historically outperformed the market in January (there is a $20 bill lying on the ground waiting to be picked up). To take advantage of this anomaly, that investor would have to buy small-cap stocks at the end of December, prior to the period of outperformance. After achieving some success with this strategy, other investors would take note—with the large dollars at stake Wall Street is quick to copy successful strategies. An academic paper might even be published. Since the effect is now known by more than just the original discoverer of the anomaly, in order to generate abnormal profits one would have to buy before others did so. Now prices start to rise in November. But the next group of investors, recognizing this was going to happen, would have to buy even earlier.

As you can see the very act of exploiting an anomaly has the effect of making it disappear, making the market more efficient. It is worth noting that if there ever was a January effect in small-cap stocks that could be exploited after the costs of the effort, it no longer exists.

The Moral of the Tale

The market may not be perfectly efficient (it is possible to find a $20 bill waiting to be picked up). The prudent investment strategy, however, is to behave as if it were. Consider carefully these words from Richard Roll, financial economist and principal of the portfolio management firm, Roll and Ross Asset Management:

> "I have personally tried to invest money, my client's and my own, in every single anomaly and predictive result that academics have dreamed up. And I have yet to make a nickel on any of these supposed market inefficiencies. An inefficiency ought to be an exploitable opportunity. If there's nothing investors can exploit in a systematic way, time in and time out, then it's very hard to say that information is not being properly incorporated into stock prices. Real money investment strategies don't produce the results that academic papers say they should."[2]

Investors who accept the EMH as fundamental to their investment strategy don't have to spend their time searching for the very few $20 bills lying on the ground. Instead, they earn market returns based on the amount of risk (their asset allocation) they are willing to accept and incur less expenses.

With the next tale we return to using an analogy to sports to teach a lesson about the belief that you can identify mutual funds that will deliver great returns by studying past returns. In other words, there is a belief that outstanding performance persists. You will see that while this is true in most endeavors (which is why it is conventional wisdom), there is no evidence of such persistence, beyond the randomly expected, among mutual funds.

Despite volumes of research attesting to the meaninglessness of past returns, most investors (and personal-finance magazines) seek tomorrow's winners among yesterday's. Forget it. The truth is, much as you may wish you could know which funds will be hot, you can't—and neither can the legions of advisers and publications that claim they can.

—*Fortune*, March 15, 1999

Chapter 4:
Persistence of Performance: Athletes Versus Investment Managers

Barry Bonds is arguably the best baseball player of his era. No one would consider him to have been lucky to generate the statistics he produced because they are persistently so much better than those of other players. What is important to understand is that his superior results are probably the result of small differences in skills. He is perhaps a bit stronger than most players (though there are some that are stronger). His bat speed is probably slightly faster (though there are others whose bat speed might be just as fast or faster). His hand/eye coordination is also probably slightly superior (again, a few probably have similar skills). He was also, at one time, one of the fastest runners in the game (though he was not that much faster than most and others had superior speed). The small differences in each of these categories (and perhaps others) allowed Bonds to be the best player in the game.

What is important to understand is that Bonds's competition is other individual players. In terms of individual skills, he is not stronger than every player. Nor is he faster than every player, and so on. The world of investing, however, presents a very different situation. And the difference in the form of competition is why we do not see persistence of outperformance of investment managers. To understand the difference we need to understand how securities markets set prices.

Dr. Mark Rubinstein, Professor of Applied Investment Analysis at the Haas School of Business at the University of California at Berkeley, provided the following insight:

> "Each investor, using the market to serve his or her own self-interest, unwittingly makes prices reflect that investor's information and analysis. It is as if the market were a huge, relatively low-cost, continuous polling mechanism that records the updated votes of millions of investors in continuously changing current prices. In light of this mechanism, for a sin-

gle investor (in the absence of inside information) to believe that prices are significantly in error is almost always folly. Public information should already be embedded in prices."[1]

Rubinstein is making the point that the competition for an investment manager is not other individual investment managers, but is instead the collective wisdom of the market—Adam Smith's famous "invisible hand." This is the same point we discussed in the sports betting story. Mark, who was an expert and wanted to bet on Duke, could not exploit his friend's lack of knowledge by giving him only thirty points. The *collective wisdom* of the market had set the point spread at forty. Thus, the competition was the market, not the skills of each individual participant.

The implication for investors, as author Ron Ross points out in *The Unbeatable Market*, is that: "The quest for market-beating strategy boils down to an information-processing contest. The entity you are competing against is the *entire* market and the accumulated information discovered by all the participants and reflected in prices."[2]

Here is another way to think about the quest for superior investment performance: "The potential for self-cancellation shows why the game of investing is so different from, for example, chess, in which even a seemingly small advantage can lead to consistent victories. Investors implicitly lump the market with other arenas of competition in their experience."[3] Rex Sinquefield, former co-chairman of Dimensional Fund Advisors (DFA) who retired in 2005, put it this way: "Just because there are some investors smarter than others, that advantage will not show up. The market is too vast and too informationally efficient."[4]

While the competition for Bonds is other individual players, the competition for investment managers is the entire market. It would be as if each time Bonds stepped up to the plate he faced a pitcher with the collective skills of Randy Johnson (fastball), Greg Maddux (control), Roger Clemens (split finger pitch), Carl Hubbell (screwball), Bert Blyleven (curveball), and Gaylord Perry (spitball). If that had been the case, Bonds certainly would not have produced the same results.

It is important to understand that the results of any game are more dependent on the skill level of the competition than on the skill of the individual competing. In the world of investing the competition is indeed tough. For example, with as much as 80 to 90 percent of the trading done by institutional investors it is difficult to think of a large enough group of likely individuals to exploit.

Understanding the true nature of the competition, and the difficulty of achieving superior performance, Ralph Wanger, former Chief Investment Officer of Liberty Wanger Asset Management and Lead Portfolio Manager of the Liberty Acorn Fund concluded:

> "For professional investors like myself, a sense of humor is essential for another reason. We are very aware that we are competing not only against the market averages but also against one another. It's an intense rivalry. We are each claiming, 'The stocks in my fund today will perform better than what you own in your fund.' That implies we think we can predict the future, which is the occupation of charlatans. If you believe you or anyone else has a system that can predict the future of the stock market, the joke is on you."[5]

There is another important difference between sports and investing that explains the lack of persistence of superior investment performance. When Bonds is up at the plate he is engaged in a zero-sum game—either he wins or the pitcher wins. As we have discussed, investment managers trying to outperform are not engaged in a zero-sum game. In their efforts to outperform the market they incur significantly higher expenses that passive investors accepting market returns. Those costs are research expenses, other fund operating expenses, bid-offer spreads, commissions, market impact costs, and taxes. It would be as if Bonds went up to the plate with a doughnut (a weight) on his bat, while all other hitters had no such handicap.

The academic research on the subject of performance persistence is clear: There is little to no evidence of any persistent ability to outperform the market without taking on greater risk.

Summary
The conventional wisdom is that past performance is a good predictor of future performance. The reason for it being conventional wisdom is that this holds true in most endeavors, be it a sporting event or any other form of competition. The problem for investors who believe in the conventional wisdom is that the nature of the competition in the investment arena is so different that the conventional wisdom does not apply—what works in one paradigm, does not necessarily work in another. Peter Bernstein, consulting editor of the *Journal of Portfolio Management* and author of several highly regarded investment books, including *Against the Gods* and *Capital Ideas*, put it this way: "In

the real world, investors seem to have great difficulty outperforming one another in any convincing or consistent fashion. Today's hero is often tomorrow's blockhead."[6]

The Moral of the Tale
To avoid choosing the wrong investment strategy one must understand the nature of the game. In the investment arena large institutional investors dominate trading. Thus, they are the ones setting prices. Therefore, the competition is tough. Making the game even more difficult is that the competition is not each individual institutional investor. Instead, it is the *collective wisdom* of all other participants. The competition is just too tough for it to be likely that any one investor will be able to persistently outperform.

The next story continues on the theme of persistence of performance.

People often see order where it doesn't exist and interpret accidental success to be the result of skill.

—Miriam Bensman, *Institutional Investor*, January 1997

Chapter 5:
The Demon of Chance

It is January 2003 and the investment committee of a large corporation meets to discuss the performance of the multi-billion dollar pension plan they are charged with overseeing. Disappointed with the performance of its investments, the committee votes to fire the manager and initiates a search for a replacement. The committee performs a thorough screening of potential candidates. Among the screens are a record of superior performance over the fifteen-year period ending in 2002, a high persistency of superior performance, tenure of the manager and turnover. The due diligence process has narrowed the final candidates to the following funds and a benchmark, the S&P 500 Index.

Fund	Annualized Returns 1988-2002 (%)
Larry Swedroe Investment Trust	14.3
Legg Mason Value	14.2
Washington Mutual	12.4
Fidelity Magellan	12.3
S&P 500 Index Fund	11.5
Janus Fund	11.3

Based on its track record the winner of the performance derby is the Larry Swedroe Investment Trust. Not only has the fund outperformed its benchmark by a significant amount, but it has also done so with a high degree of persistency, outperforming the S&P 500 Index in nine of the fifteen years (67 percent). In addition, the fund has had the same manager in charge for the entire period, and turnover has been extremely low.

After being presented with the data, the investment committee votes to award the management of the plan to the Larry Swedroe Investment Trust. At the last minute one member of the committee suggests that as one final bit of due diligence, Larry Swedroe should be brought in to explain his investment strategy.

Appearing before the committee, I am first congratulated on the superior results of the fund. I am then asked to explain my investment strategy. I respond by stating that since my wife's name is Mona, my lucky letter is M. Therefore, I construct a value-weighted portfolio of all U.S. stocks that begin with the letter M and rebalance the portfolio annually. Skill, or the demon of luck?

The above example was created by the technique known as data mining—a technique for building predictive models of the real world by discerning patterns in masses of data. The computer was asked to find a "strategy" that delivered outperformance. It then *mined the data* and found one. Before ever concluding that because a strategy worked in the past that it can be relied to work in the future, we need to ask if there is a rational explanation for the correlation between the outcome and strategy. Obviously, in the case of the Larry Swedroe Investment Trust there is no rational explanation. Thus, no rational person would engage my fund to manage assets. Unfortunately, in the real world many investment products are based on ideas that have much in common (they are the result of data mining) with the strategy of the Larry Swedroe Investment Trust.

Mutual Funds to Drool Over

The financial media are forever seeking to anoint some mutual fund manager as the financial equivalent of the Michael Jordan of investment managers—the "next Peter Lynch." They, along with many investment advisors and individual investors, perform intensive searches of databases seeking to find a fund manager with a persistent long-term record of outperformance. The assumption is that while short-term outperformance might be a matter of luck, long-term outperformance must be evidence of skill. A basic knowledge of statistics, however, provides us with the knowledge that with thousands of money managers playing the game, the odds are that a few, not just one, will produce a long-term performance record similar to that of the Larry Swedroe Investment Trust.

Coin-Tossing Gurus?

Imagine the following scenario: Ten thousand individuals are gathered together to participate in a contest. A coin will be tossed and the contestants must guess whether it will come up heads or tails. Contestants who correctly guess the outcome of ten consecutive tosses are declared winners and receive the coveted title of "coin-tossing guru."

According to statistics, we can expect that after the first toss, five thousand participants will have guessed the outcome correctly. The other five thousand will have guessed incorrectly and thus are eliminated from the competition. After the second round, the remaining participants will be expected to be 2,500; and so on. After ten repetitions we would expect to have ten remaining participants who would have guessed correctly all ten times and earned their guru status. What probability would you attach to the likelihood that those ten gurus would win the next coin-toss competition? Would you bet on them winning again? The answers are obvious.

What does this have to do with investing?

Today, there are more mutual funds than there are stocks. With so many active managers trying to win, statistical theory tells us that we should expect that some are likely to outperform the market. However, before expenses, beating the market is a zero-sum game—that is, since all stocks must be owned by someone, for every active manager who outperforms the market there must be one who underperforms. Therefore, the odds of any specific active manager being successful are at best 50/50 (before considering the burden of higher expenses active managers must overcome to outperform a benchmark index fund). Using our coin-toss analogy, we would expect that randomly half the active managers would outperform in any one year, about one in four to outperform two years in a row, and one in eight to do so three years in a row. Fund managers who outperform for even three years in a row are often declared to be gurus by the financial media. The question to consider is: Are they investment gurus or coin-tossing gurus? The answer is that it is hard to tell the difference between the two.

The reason for choosing ten thousand for the coin toss is that we are not far from having that number of actively managed funds. Using the formula from the previous example, after ten years we should randomly expect that about ten funds would outperform their benchmark every year. Without this knowledge of statistics investors are likely to confuse skill with "the demon of luck."

The latest to be acclaimed as the next Peter Lynch is Bill Miller, the manager of the Legg Mason Value Trust. He managed to do what no other current manager has done—beat the S&P 500 Index fifteen years in a row (1991–2005). Surely that cannot be luck. Surely you can rely on that performance as a predictor of future greatness. Before you come to that conclusion, consider the following evidence.

Those That Don't Know Financial History Are Doomed to Repeat It
For each of the eleven years from 1974 through 1984 the Lindner Large-Cap Fund outperformed the S&P 500 Index.[1] How were investors rewarded if they waited *eleven years* to be sure that they had found a true genius and then invested in the fund? Over the next eighteen years, the S&P 500 Index returned 12.6 percent. Believers in past performance as a prologue to future

performance were rewarded for their faith in the Lindner Large-Cap Fund with returns of just 4.1 percent, an underperformance of over 8 percent per annum for eighteen years. After outperforming for eleven years in a row, the Lindner Large-Cap Fund managed to beat the S&P 500 in just four of the next eighteen years, and none of the last nine—quite a price to pay for believing that past performance is a predictor of future performance. The Lindner Fund was finally put out of its misery when it was purchased by the Hennessy Funds in October 2003 and eventually merged into the Hennessy Total Return Fund.

Not yet convinced? Consider the case of David Baker, and the 44 Wall Street Fund. Over the entire decade of the 1970s, 44 Wall Street was the top-performing diversified U.S. stock fund—even outperforming the legendary Peter Lynch who ran Fidelity's Magellan Fund. Faced with the decision of which fund to invest in, why would anyone settle for Peter Lynch when they could have David Baker? (We only know after the fact that Lynch continued to achieve superior results in the 1980s.)

How did investors fare after waiting ten years to be sure that David Baker's results had to be the result of skill and not random good luck? Unfortunately, 44 Wall Street ranked as the single worst performing fund of the 1980s, losing 73 percent.[2] During the same period, the S&P 500 grew 17.6 percent per annum. Each dollar invested in Baker's fund fell in value to just twenty-seven cents. On the other hand, each dollar invested in the S&P 500 Index would have grown to just over five dollars. The fund did so poorly that in 1993 it was merged into the 44 Wall Street Equity Fund, which was then merged into the Matterhorn Growth Fund in 1996.

The Moral of the Tale

As evidenced by the examples of the Linder Large-Cap Fund and the 44 Wall Street Fund, belief in the "hot hand" and past performance as a predictor of the future performance of actively managed funds and their managers can be quite expensive. Unfortunately, both the financial media and the public are quick to assume that superior performance is a result of skill rather than the more likely assumption that it was a random outcome. The reason is that noise sells, and the financial media is in the business of selling. They are not in the business of providing prudent investment advice.

The bottom line is that while there will likely be future Peter Lynchs and future Bill Millers, we have no way to identify them ahead of time. Also, unfortunately, we can only buy future performance, not past performance. A perfect example of this obvious truism is that in 2006, Miller's streak was broken as the Legg Mason Value Trust underperformed the S&P 500 Index by almost 10 percent. In fact, the fund's performance was so poor that its cumulative three-year returns trailed the S&P 500 Index by 2.8 percent per annum. This provides further evidence of the fact that it is extremely difficult to tell whether past performance was the result of skill or the "demon of luck."

The conclusion that we can draw is that while relying on past performance as a guide to the future might lead you to investing with the next Peter Lynch, it is just as likely to lead you to investing with the next David Baker. That is a risk that a prudent, risk-averse investor (probably you) should not be willing to accept. If you do accept that risk it is likely that you will be reciting the investor's lament: "I own last year's top performing funds. Unfortunately, I bought them this year." Investors interested in learning how easy it is to be fooled by what are often random outcomes would be well served to read *Fooled by Randomness*, an excellent book by Nassim Nicholas Taleb.

The next story focuses on choosing the winning strategy in the face of uncertainty.

I believe the search for top-performing stock funds is an intellectually discredited exercise that will come to be viewed as one of the great financial follies of the late 20th century.

—Jonathan Clements

Chapter 6:
When Even the Best Aren't Likely to Win the Game

A wizard appears, waves his magic wand, and makes you the eleventh best golfer in the world. Being the eleventh best golfer in the world earns you an invitation to the annual Super Legends of Golf Tournament. That is the good news. The bad news is that the competition is the ten best players in the world. To even the playing field you are given a major advantage. The rules of the game are as follows. Each of the other players will play one hole at a time and then return to the clubhouse and report his score. No player gets to observe the others play. Thus, you cannot gain an advantage by watching the others play. After each of the other ten players completes the hole you are provided with the following options. Option A is to choose to play the hole and accept whatever score you obtain. Option B is to choose not to play that hole and accept par as your score.

The first hole is a par four. After each of the ten best players in the world has completed the first hole you learn that eight of the ten took five shots to put the ball in the cup—they shot a bogie. Two players shot birdies, needing only three shots to put the ball in the cup. You now must decide to either accept par or play the hole. What is your decision?

The prudent choice would be to choose not to play, take par, and accept a score of four. The logic is that while it was not impossible to beat par (two players did) the odds of doing so are so low (20 percent) that it would not be prudent to try. And by accepting par you would have outperformed 80 percent of the best players in the world. In other words, when the best players in the world fail the majority of the time, you recognize that it is not prudent to try to succeed. The exception to this line of thinking would be if you could somehow identify an advantage you might have.

For example, if the ten best players had played the day before you in a rainstorm, with fifty-mile-an-hour winds, and you played the following day when the weather was perfect and the course was dry. Given that situation you might decide that the advantage was great enough that the odds of your shooting a birdie (a three) were greater than the odds of your shooting a bogie (a five, or perhaps even worse). Without such an advantage the prudent choice would be to not play if you don't have to.

What does this story have to do with investing? Consider the following. It seems logical to believe that if anyone could beat the market, it would be the pension plans of the largest U.S. companies. Why is this a good assumption? First, these pension plans control large sums of money. They have access to the best and brightest portfolio managers, each clamoring to manage the billions of dollars in these plans (and earn large fees). Pension plans can also invest with managers that most individuals don't have access to because they don't have sufficient assets to meet the minimums of these superstar managers.

Second, it is not even remotely possible that these pension plans ever hired a manager who did not have a track record of outperforming their benchmarks, or at the very least matching them. Certainly they would never hire a manager with a record of underperformance.

Third, it is also safe to say that they never hired a manager who did not make a great presentation, explaining why the manager had succeeded, and why she would continue to succeed. Surely the case presented was a convincing one.

Fourth, many, if not the majority, of these pension plans hire professional consultants such as Frank Russell, SEI, and Goldman Sachs, to help them perform due diligence in interviewing, screening, and ultimately selecting the very best of the best. Frank Russell, for example, has boasted that they have over seventy analysts performing over two thousand interviews a year. And you can be sure that these consultants have thought of every conceivable screen to find the best fund managers. Surely they have considered not only performance records, but also such factors as management tenure, depth of staff, consistency of performance (to make sure that a long-term record is not the result of one or two lucky years), performance in bear markets, consistency of implementation of strategy, turnover, costs, etc. It is unlikely that there is something that you or your financial advisor would think of that they had not already considered.

Fifth, as individuals, it is rare that we would have the luxury of being able to personally interview money managers and perform as thorough a due diligence as do these consultants. And we generally don't have professionals helping us to avoid mistakes in the process. As individuals we are generally stuck relying on Morningstar's ratings; and despite the tremendous resources that Morningstar employs in the effort to identify future winners, its track record is poor. For example, *The Hulbert Financial Digest* tracked the performance of Morningstar's five-star funds for the period 1993–2000. For that eight-year period the total return (pretax) on Morningstar's top-rated U.S.

funds averaged +106 percent. This compared to a total return of +222 percent for the total stock market, as measured by the Wilshire 5000 Equity Index. Hulbert also found that the top-rated funds, while achieving less than 50 percent of the market's return, carried a relative risk (measured by standard deviation) that was 26 percent greater than that of the market.[1] If the performance had been measured on an after-tax basis, the tax inefficiency of actively managed funds relative to a passive index fund would have made the comparison significantly worse.

Hulbert also looked at a portfolio consisting of only Morningstar's highest rated funds, as highlighted in Morningstar's newsletter. How did such a portfolio fare? From January 1999 through March 2002, it trailed the market by almost 6 percent per annum, after paying sales charges, redemption fees and other transaction costs.[2] And finally, for the period 1995–2001, funds rated one star outperformed funds rated five star by 45 percent.[3]

Returning to our golf story, I hope you agree that just as it would be imprudent to try to beat par when 80 percent of the best golfers in the world failed, it would be imprudent for you to try to succeed if institutional investors, with far greater resources than you (or your broker or financial advisor), had also failed about 80 percent of the time. The only exception would be if you could identify a strategic advantage that you had over these institutional players. The questions you might ask yourself are: Do I have more resources than they do? Do I have more time to spend finding future winners than they do? Am I smarter than all of these institutional investors and the advisors they hire? Unless when you look in the mirror you see Warren Buffet staring back at you, it doesn't seem likely that the answer to any of these questions is yes. At least it won't be yes if you are honest with yourself. So let's now turn to the evidence and see just how these institutional investors fare at beating par.

The Evidence

The consulting firm FutureMetrics studied the performance of approximately two hundred major U.S. corporate pension plans for the seventeen-year period 1988–2004.[4] Since it is estimated that the average pension plan has an allocation of 60 percent equities and 40 percent fixed income, we can compare the realized returns of these plans to a benchmark portfolio with an asset allocation of 60 percent S&P 500 Index and 40 percent Lehman Brothers Intermediate Government/Corporate Bond Index. This passive portfolio could have been implemented by each of the plans as an alternative to active strategies. If the return did not match the return of the indexes (less some low expenses), it must be that the players were trying to shoot birdies while running the risk of shooting bogies—they must have been engaging in active management. Unfortunately, only about 20 percent of the pension plans playing the game of attempting to outperform the market succeeded. Each pension plan obviously believed that they were likely to outperform. If this were not the case, why would they have played? Unfortunately, in a colossal triumph of hope over experience (and perhaps the all-too-human trait of overconfidence), 80 percent failed in the attempt to beat par. Eighty percent shot bogies.

It is important to understand that by trying to be above average (beat par), 80 percent of the players produced returns that were below their benchmark. It is also important to acknowledge that it is unlikely that the failure occurred because of poor corporate governance.

Based on my experience, it is safe to say that the investment policy committee members considered themselves good stewards. In other words, they were smart people who performed their roles diligently—yet 80 percent of the time they failed. And with 80 percent failing it is unlikely that they failed because of bad luck. If it was not bad luck, and it was not failure of process, what led to such a high failure rate? The answer is that the strategy they used—active management—was a losing strategy. This did not have to be so.

Just as you prudently chose not to play the first hole of the Super Legends of Golf Tournament, they too could have chosen not to play by investing instead in index funds. By doing so, they would have earned par.

The story is actually worse than even these dismal results suggest. Consider that a large number of these pension plans invested at least some small portion of their plans in such riskier asset classes as small-cap and value stocks, junk bonds, venture capital, and emerging market equities. As higher-risk asset classes, they have higher expected returns. Yet despite this advantage, for the time period surveyed, 80 percent of the funds failed to beat par. These pension plans were actually taking more risk and they earned lower, not higher, returns.

Consider also that since the average pension plan has an allocation of 60 percent equities and 40 percent bonds, some surely have a higher allocation. Given that equities outperformed bonds over the period of the study, any plan with an allocation of more than 60 percent stocks would have had an advantage. It would be as if these plans teed off from the yellow tee (the tee from which women hit), while the indexers teed off from the blue tee (the tee from which highest level of men hit). Yet despite these advantages, just 20 percent succeeded. Again, these plans were taking more risk but were "rewarded" with lower returns.

Ask yourself what advantage you have that would allow you to have a high degree of confidence that you would be likely to succeed where the best failed 80 percent of the time.

You should also consider the following. Within the last fifteen years, Intel, Exxon Mobil, Philip Morris, and the Washington State Investment Board, with combined assets of about $60 billion, have fired all the active fund managers they had previously hired. Surely, it is safe to assume that none of these plans ever hired a manager with a poor performance record. Yet each of them fired all of the managers that they had hired after a thorough due diligence process. Why were the managers all fired? Is it even remotely possible that they were fired because they outperformed? Of course not. Thus, we can safely assume that while the active managers were hired with the expectation of outperformance, the reality did not live up to the expectation.

In 1996, Philip Halpern was the chief investment officer of the Washington State Investment Board (a large institutional investor). He and two of his coworkers wrote an article on their investment experiences. They wrote the article because their experience with active management was less than satisfactory and they knew, through their attendance at professional associations, that many of their colleagues shared, and therefore corroborated, their own experience. The article included a quote from a Goldman Sachs publication: "Few managers consistently outperform the S&P 500. Thus, in the eyes of the plan sponsor, its plan is paying an excessive amount of the upside to the manager while still bearing substantial risk that its investments will achieve sub-par returns." The article concluded, "Slowly, over time, many large pension funds have shared our experience and have moved toward indexing more domestic equity assets."[5]

Returning again to our golf analogy, we determined that while it might be possible to shoot a birdie, it was not prudent for you to try. The reason is that you could not identify an advantage that would lead you to believe that you would be likely to outperform the best. The risk-to-reward ratio was poor—80 percent failed. We have seen that the same thing is true in investing—80 percent of the very best hit bogies.

The Moral of the Tale

Wall Street needs and wants you to play the game of active investing. They need you to try to beat par. They know that your odds of success are so low that it is not in your interest to play. But they need you to play so that *they* (not you) make the most money. They make it by charging high fees for active management that persistently delivers poor performance.

The financial media also want and need you to play so that you "tune in."

That is how *they* (not you) make money. However, just as you had the choice of not playing in the Super Legends of Golf Tournament, you have the choice of not playing the game of active management. You can simply accept par and earn market (not average) rates of return with low expenses and high tax efficiency. You can do so by investing in passively managed investment vehicles like index funds and passive asset class funds. By doing so, you are virtually guaranteed to outperform the majority of both professionals and individual investors. In other words, you win by not playing. This is why active investing is called the loser's game. It is not that the people playing are losers. And it is not that you cannot win. Instead, it is that the odds of success are so low that it is imprudent to try.

The only logical reason to play the game of active investing is that you place a high entertainment value on the effort. For some people there might even be another reason—they enjoy the bragging rights if they win. Of course you rarely, if ever, hear when they lose.

Yes active investing is exciting. Investing, however, was never meant to be exciting. Wall Street and the media created that myth. Instead, it is meant to be about providing you with the greatest odds of achieving your financial goals with the least amount of risk. That is what differentiates investing from speculating (gambling).

Many people get excitement from gambling on sporting events, horse races or at the casino tables in Las Vegas. Prudent individuals, however, get entertainment value from gambling by betting only an infinitesimal fraction of their net worth on sporting events, etc. Similarly, even if you receive entertainment value from the pursuit of the "Holy Grail of Outperformance," you should not gamble more than a tiny fraction of the assets on which you wish to retire (or leave to your children or favorite charity) on active managers being able to overcome such great odds.

The following words of wisdom from Daniel Kahneman, professor of psychology and public affairs at Princeton University, are a fitting conclusion to this story.

> "What's really quite remarkable in the investment world is that people are playing a game which, in some sense, cannot be played. There are so many people out there in the market; the idea that any single individual without extra information or extra market power can beat the market is extraordinarily unlikely. Yet the market is full of people who think they can do it and full of other people who believe them. This is one

of the great mysteries of finance: Why do people believe they can do the impossible? And why do other people believe them?"[6]

The next tale also demonstrates the point that often it is more prudent to not play than to play.

The greatest advantage from gambling comes from not playing it at all.

—Girolamo Cardano, sixteenth century physician, mathematician, and quintessential Renaissance man

Chapter 7:
Outfoxing the Box

My good friend Bill Schultheis, author of *The Coffeehouse Investor*, devised "Outfoxing the Box" to help investors understand that the winning investment strategy is to accept market returns. Like our golfing example, it depicts a game that you can choose to either play or not play.

In this game you are an investor with the following choice to make. The table below contains nine percentages, each representing a rate of return your financial assets are guaranteed to earn for the rest of your life.

%	%	%
0	5	23
6	**10**	14
-3	15	20

You are told that you have the following choice: You can either accept the 10 percent rate of return in the center box or you will be asked to leave the room, the boxes will be shuffled around, and you will have to choose a box, not knowing what return each box holds. You quickly calculate that the average return of the other eight boxes is 10 percent. Thus, if thousands of people played the game and each one chose a box, the expected average return would be the same as if they all chose not to play. Of course, some would earn a return of negative 3 percent per annum, while others would earn 23 percent per annum. This is like the world of investing, where if you chose an actively managed fund and the market returns 10 percent, you might be lucky and earn as much as 23 percent per annum; or you might be unlucky and lose 3 percent per annum. A rational risk-averse investor should logically decide to "outfox the box" and accept the average (market) return of 10 percent.

In my years as an investment advisor, whenever I present this game to an investor, I have never once had an investor choose to play. Everyone chooses to accept par, or 10 percent. While they might be willing to spend a dollar on a lottery ticket, they become more prudent in their choice when it comes to investing their life's savings.

Now consider the following. In the "outfoxing the box" game, the *average* return of all choices was the same 10 percent as the 10 percent that would have been earned by choosing not to play. And 50 percent of those choosing to play would be expected to earn an above-average return and 50 percent a below-average return. As we saw in the prior tale, the real world study on the returns of pension plans demonstrated that among supposedly sophisticated institutional investors, with access to all the great money managers in the world, about 80 percent of the players received a below-market return and thus would have been better off not playing. If you would choose to not play a game when you have a 50 percent chance of success, what logic is there in choosing to play a game where the most sophisticated investors have an 80 percent rate of failure? Yet that is exactly the choice those playing the game of active management are making. They are choosing to play the game of outfoxing the box, even when seven of the nine (78 percent) boxes have below average returns!

You have seen the evidence on how poor the odds of success are for the professional investors—those big institutional pension plans with all of their resources. In addition to their other advantages, institutional investors have one other major advantage over individual investors—their returns are not subject to taxes. However, if your equity investments are in a taxable account, the returns you earn are subject to taxes. Let's look then at the odds of success of outperforming par (a simple indexing strategy) for those individuals who invest in actively managed mutual funds.

The study titled "How Well Have Taxable Investors Been Served in the 1980s and 1990s?" investigated the likelihood of after-tax outperformance.[1] The benchmark used was Vanguard's S&P 500 Index Fund. For the twenty-year period from 1979 to 1998, just 14 percent of the funds outperformed their benchmark on an after-tax basis. And, importantly, the average after-tax outperformance was just 1.3 percent per annum. On the other hand, the average after-tax underperformance by the 86 percent that failed to beat par was 3.2 percent annum. In other words, if you had chosen to play that game you had a slim chance of winning, and even when you did succeed you only would likely have won a relatively small amount. On the other hand, you faced the high likelihood of failure. And when you did fail, you underperformed by a large amount.

It would be as if in our golf story instead of eight of the ten golfers shooting bogies (fives) they would have shot triple bogies (sevens). Since no one would choose to play the game when 80 percent of the best players shot bogies, the logic of taking par becomes even more powerful if they were to shoot triple bogies. The conclusion of the study was that the high odds of failure with large losses combined with low odds of success with small gains produced risk-adjusted odds against outperformance of over *fifteen to one*.

The story is actually even worse than it appears because the data above contains survivorship bias. Thirty-three funds disappeared during the time frame covered by the study. Thus, the risk-adjusted odds of outperformance are even lower than the dismal figure previously presented.

The Moral of the Tale

You don't have to play the game of active investing. You don't have to try to overcome abysmal odds—odds that make the crap tables at Las Vegas seem appealing. Instead, you can outfox the box and accept market returns by investing passively. Charles Ellis, author of *Investment Policy: How to Win the Loser's Game*, put it this way: "In investment management, the real opportunity to achieve superior results is not in scrambling to outperform the market, but in establishing and adhering to appropriate investment policies over the long term—policies that position the portfolio to benefit from riding with the main long-term forces in the market."[2]

The next story demonstrates just how strong the conventional wisdom is on past performance being a predictor of the future.

The definition of insanity is doing the same thing over and over and expecting different results.

—Benjamin Franklin

Chapter 8:
Between a Rock and a Hard Place

According to Greek mythology, Sisyphus was the son of Aeolus (the king of Thessaly). Sisyphus was a clever and evil man, who would waylay travelers and murder them. He also betrayed the secrets of the gods and bound Thanatos, the god of death, so the deceased could not reach the underworld. Hades eventually intervened, severely punishing Sisyphus. He was forced to remain in the realm of the dead and complete the same task for eternity. The task — push a boulder up a steep hill only to watch the boulder roll back down just before it reaches the top. Then he must begin the whole process again. Are investors who search for outperformance via active management condemned to a similar fate?

The majority of financial advisors, investment policy committees, and trustees of pension and retirements plans select investment managers based on historical performance. The selection process includes thorough due diligence, often with the assistance of a "gatekeeper"—a consulting firm such as Frank Russell or SEI. These firms have tremendous resources. Unfortunately, on average, the active managers chosen based on outstanding track records have failed to live up to expectations. The underperformance relative to passive benchmarks invariably leads decision-makers to fire the active manager. And the process begins anew. A new round of due diligence is performed and a new manager is selected to replace the poorly performing one. And, almost invariably, the process is repeated a few years later. Individual investors go through the same motions. And end up with the same results—a high likelihood of poor performance.

The conventional wisdom that past performance is a great predictor of future performance is so strongly ingrained in our culture it seems that almost no one ever stops to ask if the conventional wisdom is correct, even in the face of persistent failure. Why aren't investors asking themselves "If the process I used to choose a manager that would deliver outperformance failed, and I use the exact same process the next time, why should I expect anything but failure the next time?" The answer is painfully obvious. If you don't do anything different, you should expect the same result. Yet, so many have not thought to ask this most simple of questions.

It is important to understand that neither the purveyors of active management nor the gatekeepers want you to ask that question. If you did, they would go out of business. You, on the other hand, should ask that question. Your obligation is to provide the best returns, either to yourself or to members of the plan for which you are a trustee, not to provide the fund managers with a living.

As Director of Research for Buckingham Asset Management, I have asked hundreds of people this simple question, and not once have I ever received an answer that explains either why they should expect a different outcome, or what they will be doing different this time to avoid the prior outcome. It is as if those who select active managers believe that they will be able to "push Sisyphus's rock over the top of the mountain."

The Moral of the Tale

Like Sisyphus, both individual and institutional investors seem condemned to a life of repeating an action that is doomed to fail—though the odds are not quite as bad as they are for Sisyphus. As the story goes, Sisyphus is doomed to a failure rate of 100 percent. The evidence for investors is that over the long term, choosing active managers only fails about 80 percent of the time. Of course it doesn't have to be that way. Investors would benefit from taking George Santayana's advice: "Those who cannot remember the past are condemned to repeat it."

The next story focuses on debunking one of the greatest investment fables.

Investors must keep in mind that there's a difference between a good company and a good stock. After all, you can buy a good car but pay too much for it.

—Loren Fox

Chapter 9:
Great Companies Do Not Make
High-Return Investments

It is New Year's Day 1964. John Doe is the greatest security analyst in the world. He is able to identify, with uncanny accuracy, the companies that will produce high rates of return on assets over the next forty years. Unlike real world analysts and investors, he never makes a mistake in forecasting which companies will produce great earnings.

In the history of the world there has never been such an analyst. Even Warren Buffett has made mistakes, investing in companies like U.S. Air and Salomon Brothers.

While John cannot see into the future as it pertains to the *stock prices* of those companies, following the *conventional wisdom* of Wall Street he builds a portfolio of the stocks of these great companies. He does so because he has confidence that since these are going to be great-performing companies they will make great investments. Relating this to our sports betting story, he has identified the Dukes of the investment world. We can identify these great companies ourselves by the fact that growth companies have high price-to-earnings ratios.

Jane Smith, on the other hand, believes that markets are efficient. She bases her strategy on the theory that if the market believes that a group of companies will produce superior results, the market must also believe that they are relatively safe investments. With this knowledge, investors (the market) will already have bid up the price of those stocks to reflect those great expectations and the low level of perceived risk. While the *companies* are likely to produce great financial results, the *stocks* of these great companies are likely to produce relatively low returns. Jane, expecting (though not being certain) that the market will reward her for taking risk, instead buys a passively managed portfolio of the stocks of value, or distressed, companies. She even anticipates the likelihood that, on average, these *companies* will continue to be relatively poor performers. Despite this expectation, she does expect the *stocks* to provide superior returns, thereby rewarding her for taking risk. We can identify these companies by their low price-to-earnings ratios.

As you will see, Jane believes that markets work — they are efficient.

John does not. Relating this to our sports betting story, John believes that you can bet on Duke and not have to give any points when they play Army.

Faced with the choice of buying the stocks of "great" companies or buying the stocks of "lousy" companies, most investors would instinctively choose the former. Before looking at the historical evidence, ask yourself what would you do? Assuming your only objective is to achieve high returns, regardless of the risk entailed, would you buy the stocks of the great companies or the stocks of the lousy companies?

Let us now jump forward to 2006. How did John's and Jane's investment strategies work out? Who was right? In a sense, they were both right. For the forty-two-year period ending in 2005, the return on assets (ROA) for John's great growth stocks was 9.3 percent per year. This was over twice the 4.0 percent ROA for Jane's lousy value stocks. The average annual return to investors in Jane's value stocks was, however, 16.1 percent per annum—49 percent greater than the 10.8 percent average annual return to investors in John's great growth stocks.

If the major purpose of investment research is to determine which companies will be the great performing companies, and when you are correct in your analysis you produce inferior results, why bother? Why not save the time and the expense and just let the markets reward you for taking risk?

Small Companies versus Large Companies

If the theory that markets provide returns commensurate with the amount of risk taken holds true, one should expect to see similar results if Jane invested in a passively managed portfolio consisting of small companies that are intuitively riskier than large companies. For example, small companies don't have the economies of scale that large companies have, making them generally less efficient. They typically have weaker balance sheets and fewer sources of capital. When there is distress in the capital markets, smaller companies are generally the first ones to be cut off from access to capital, increasing the risk of bankruptcy. They don't have the depth of management that larger companies do. They generally don't have long track records from which investors can make judgments. The cost of trading small stocks is much greater, increasing the risk of investing in them. And so on.

When one compares the performance of the asset class of small companies with the performance of the large company asset class one gets the same results produced by the great company versus value company comparison. For the same forty-two-year period ending in 2005, while small companies produced returns on assets almost 40 percent below those of large companies (6.0

percent versus 3.7 percent), the annual average investment return on the stocks of small companies exceeded the return on stocks of large companies by about 36 percent (16.1 percent versus 11.8 percent). What seems to be an anomaly actually makes the point that markets work. The riskier investment in small companies produced higher returns.

Why Great Earnings Don't Translate Into Great Investment Returns
The simple explanation for this anomaly is that investors discount the future expected earnings of value stocks at a higher rate than they discount the future earnings of growth stocks. This more than offsets the faster earnings growth rates of growth companies. The high discount rate results in low current valuations for value stocks and higher expected future returns relative to growth stocks. Why do investors use a higher discount rate for value stocks when calculating the current value? The following example should provide a clear explanation.

Let's consider the case of two identical (except for location) office buildings that are for sale in your town. Property A is in the heart of the most desirable commercial area, while Property B borders the worst slum in the region. Clearly it is easy to identify the more desirable property. (Just as it is easy to identify that Duke is better than Army.) If you could buy either property at $10 million, the obvious choice would be Property A. This world, therefore, could not exist. If it did, investors would bid up the price of Property A relative to Property B.

Now let's imagine a slightly more realistic scenario, one in which Property A is selling at $20 million and Property B at $5 million. Based on the projected rental cash flows, you project that (by coincidence) both properties will provide an expected rate of return of 10 percent—the higher rental income tenants pay for the better location is exactly offset by the higher price you have to pay to buy the property. Faced with the choice of which property to buy, the rational choice is still Property A. The reason is that it provides the same expected return as Property B while being a less risky investment. Being able to buy the safer investment at the same expected return as a riskier one would be like being able to bet on Duke to beat Army and not have to give away any points. Thus, this world could not exist either.

In the real world Property A's price would continue to be bid up relative to Property B's. Perhaps Property A's price might rise to $30 million and Property B's might fall to $4 million. Now Property A's expected rate of return is lower than Property B's. Investors demand a higher expected return for taking more risk. It is important to understand that the fact that Property A provides a lower expected rate of return than Property B does not make it a worse investment choice—just a safer one. The market views it as less risky and thus discounts its future earnings at a lower rate. The result is that the price of Property A is driven up, which in turn lowers its expected return. The price differential between the two will reflect the perceived differences in risk. Risk and *ex-ante* reward must be related. The way to think about this is that the market drives prices until the *risk-adjusted* returns are equal. It is true that Property B has higher expected returns. However, we must adjust those higher expected returns for the greater risk entailed.

Most everyone understands the relationship between risk and expected return in the context of this example. However, it always amazes me that this most basic of principles is almost universally forgotten when thinking about stocks and how they are priced by the market.

With this understanding, we can now complete the picture by considering the case of two similar companies, Wal-Mart and JC Penney. Think of Wal-Mart as Property A and JC Penney as Property B. Most investors would say that Wal-Mart is a better company and a safer investment. Another way to think about the two companies is that Wal-Mart is Duke and JC Penney is Army. If an investor could buy either company at the same market capitalization, say $20 billion, the obvious choice would be Wal-Mart. It would be like betting on Duke and not having to give away any points. Wal-Mart not only has higher current earnings, but it is also expected to produce a faster growth of earnings. If this world existed, investors owning shares in JC Penney would immediately sell those shares in order to be able to buy shares in Wal-Mart. Their actions would drive up the price of Wal-Mart and drive down the price of JC Penney. This would result in lowering the risk premium demanded by investors in Wal-Mart and raising it on JC Penney.

Now let us say that Wal-Mart's price rises relative to JC Penney. Wal-Mart is now selling at $100 billion and JC Penney at $10 billion. At this point the two have the same *expected* (not guaranteed) future rate of return—say 10 percent. Given that Wal-Mart is perceived to be the better company, and therefore a less risky investment, investors should still choose Wal-Mart. The reason is that although we now have equal expected returns, there is less perceived risk in owning Wal-Mart. So our process of investors buying Wal-Mart and selling JC Penney continues.

It does so until the expected return of owning JC Penney is sufficiently greater than the expected return of owning Wal-Mart to entice investors to accept the risk of owning JC Penney instead of owning Wal-Mart—say a price of $200 billion for Wal-Mart and $5 billion for JC Penney. The size of the differential (and thus the difference in future expected returns) between the price of the stocks of Wal-Mart and JC Penney will be directly related to the difference in perceived investment risk. Given that Wal-Mart is perceived to be a much safer investment than JC Penney, the price differential (risk premium) may have to be very large to entice investors to accept the risk of owning JC Penney—just as the point spread between Duke and Army has to be very large in order to entice "investors" to take the risk of betting on Army.

Would these price changes make Wal-Mart "overvalued" or "highly valued" relative to JC Penney? The answer is "highly valued." Just as in the case of Duke being favored by forty points over Army, Duke is not overvalued—it is highly valued. If investors thought Wal-Mart was overvalued relative to JC Penney, they would sell Wal-Mart and buy JC Penney until equilibrium was reached. Instead, the high relative valuation of Wal-Mart reflects low perceived risk. Wal-Mart's future earnings are being discounted at a low rate, reflecting the low perceived risk. This low discount rate translates into low future expected returns. Risk and reward are directly related, at least in terms of expected future returns—"expected" since we cannot know the future with certainty. JC Penney's future earnings are discounted at a high rate. It, therefore, has a relatively low valuation, reflecting the greater perceived risk. However, it also has high expected future returns.

Just as Property A is not a bad investment (it is a safe one) and Property B is not a good investment (it is a risky one), Wal-Mart is not a bad investment (it is a safe one) and JC Penney is not a good investment (it is a risky one). Once we adjust for risk, the expected returns are the same, and they are equally good (or bad) investments.

The Moral of the Tale
There is a simple principle to remember that can help you avoid making poor investment decisions. Risk and *expected* return should be positively related. Value stocks have provided a large and persistent premium over growth stocks for a logical reason—value stocks are the stocks of risky companies. That is why their stock prices are distressed. Investors refuse to buy them unless the prices are driven *low enough* so that they can expect to earn a *rate of return* that is *high enough* to compensate them for investing in risky companies. For similar reasons small stocks have also provided a risk premium relative to large stocks.

Remember, if prices are high, they reflect low perceived risk, and thus you should expect low future returns; and vice versa. This does not make a highly priced stock a poor investment. It simply makes it an investment that is perceived to have low risk and thus low future returns. Thinking otherwise would be like assuming government bonds are poor investments when the alternative is junk bonds.

The next story tackles another bit of conventional wisdom—that stocks are only risky if your investment horizon is short.

There are well-dressed foolish ideas just as there are well-dressed fools.

—Nicholas Chamfort

Chapter 10:
Stocks for the Long Run

It was January 1, 2000. As he did each year on this day Sammy sat down to review his investment plan. He was forty-five years old and planned to retire in twenty years. As a Christmas gift Sammy had received a copy of Jeremy Siegel's (finance professor at the University of Pennsylvania's Wharton School of Business) highly acclaimed book *Stocks for the Long Run* and read it over the holidays. What Sammy learned from the book was that stocks were not risky if your investment horizon was sufficiently long. He learned that stocks had always outperformed bonds as long as your investment horizon was long enough, say ten or twenty years.

Up until this point, Sammy had been a fairly conservative investor. He had maintained an asset allocation of 50 percent stocks and 50 percent bonds. The evidence in *Stocks For the Long Run*, however, convinced Sammy that since his investment horizon was at least twenty years (he wasn't planning on dying at age sixty-five) he should invest 100 percent of his assets in the stock market. He was a patient investor and was tired of missing out on the spectacular returns his friends had earned in the prior decade when the S&P 500 Index had provided a return of over 18 percent per annum—and many of his friends had done even better investing in technology stocks. So Sammy sold all his bonds and invested the proceeds in a variety of mutual funds that were large-cap and growth oriented, including a significant allocation to the technology sector. After all, those funds invested in the greatest companies in the world.

The following New Year's Day, Sammy reviewed his brokerage statements and found that his all-stock portfolio had fallen about 15 percent. Out of curiosity he went and checked how the bond funds he had sold had performed and found that they had actually risen over 10 percent. The stocks he bought underperformed the bonds he sold by about 25 percent. While not happy, he did recall the evidence from the book he had read. He was determined to be patient and stay the course.

On January 1, 2002, Sammy again reviewed his financial statements. He found that his all-equity portfolio had once again fallen sharply. And this time it was even worse. His portfolio had lost over 20 percent in just one year. Cumulatively he had now lost a full one-third of his assets. If that was not painful enough, Sammy once again checked to see how the bond funds he had sold had performed. He found that once again they had risen—this time by just under 10 percent. It was starting to get to him that while the equities he had bought had lost one-third of their value, the bonds he had sold had appreciated about 20 percent. Some quick math resulted in the disturbing finding that the equity funds he had bought would have to rise about 80 percent just to catch up with the bond funds he had sold—and that was if the bond funds provided no return at all.

Sammy was still determined to stay the course. He thought, I have already sustained the big losses and if I sell now I won't ever be able to recover. And he remembered some advisor saying that losses are only losses if you sell—stocks always win in the long run. And, after all, it really could not get any worse. And Sammy recalled that after the two-year bear market that ran from 1973 through 1974 the market went on a bull run. In 1975 the S&P 500 Index rose 37 percent and in 1976 it rose another 24 percent. Sammy did not want to take his losses only to witness a repeat of that performance. He once again decided to stay the course.

Forward to January 1, 2003. Sammy again performed his annual portfolio review. While he thought it could not get any worse, it had actually gotten far worse. The bear market of 2000 through 2001 had turned into the greatest bear market for large-cap growth stocks since the Great Depression. His equity portfolio had fallen another 22 percent and had now lost a cumulative total of almost 50 percent. A glutton for punishment, Sammy could not resist checking how those conservative bond funds he had sold had performed. He found that they had once again risen, this time by about 5 percent. While his equities had lost about one-half their value, those staid bond funds he had sold had risen about 25 percent in value. Doing some quick math he found that the stock funds he owned would now have to outperform the bond funds he had sold by about 125 percent just to catch up, let alone compensate him for all the risk he had taken—or for the stomach acid he had endured.

While Sammy was a patient and disciplined investor he was beginning to question the wisdom of his decision to abandon the more conservative strategy he had followed for over twenty years—one that had served him well. He was also concerned that if the market continued to fall he would never be able to retire, let alone retire at age sixty-five. Sammy thought the smart thing to do was to do some further research. What if stocks did not always outperform bonds at horizons as long as even twenty years (and he now only had seventeen left before retirement). The first thing he did was go to the library to check the historical record.

From his research Sammy found that for the *twenty-three* year period

1966–88, the U.S. large-cap growth stocks in which he was invested had underperformed totally riskless one-month bank certificates of deposit. The stocks of the great growth companies had earned just 7.7 percent per annum over that twenty-three year period while those totally riskless CDs were returning 8.4 percent per annum. And over that same period, five-year government bonds, the kind he had traditionally invested in, also outperformed those great growth stocks, providing a return of 8 percent.

Sammy was now concerned. Could it be that stocks really were risky, no matter the length of your investment horizon? Sammy decided to talk to his neighbor and good friend Hideki. Hideki came to the United States from Japan in 1990 to run the New York office of Nomura Securities, a large Japanese investment firm. Sammy knew that Hideki was an expert on investing. He thought that if anyone would know the answer to the question he would. So on the way home he stopped off at Hideki's apartment.

Hideki related the following story. "At the time I came to the United States the Japanese economy was dominating the world. Japanese stocks had returned over 20 percent per annum for the prior two decades. With the strongest economy in the world I was sure that Japanese stocks not only would continue to deliver superior returns, but that they were also the safest investments in the world. So I decided to keep all of my assets in Japanese stocks. At the time the Nikkei Index was at about 40,000." Hideki sighed, took a deep breath, and continued.

He said, "It's now 2003. After all these years the Nikkei is still down about 75 percent. I am resigned to never recovering my losses. I am also resigned to the fact that I cannot retire as planned. Whoever told you stocks are not risky if your horizon is long enough has not studied his history. In fact, that was the mistake I made. Despite being in the investment business, I too had forgotten my history. Consider this, Sammy. In 1900 the Egyptian stock market was one of the largest in the world. More than one hundred years later, it is likely that most of those investors never saw a return *of* their capital, let alone a return *on* their capital."

He concluded, "Sammy, none of us knows the future. The problem with the advice you got from that book was that its advice relied on a limited sample—the history of U.S. stocks for a relatively short period. The sample was also biased in that it looked only at the returns from a winner. And there was never any guarantee that the future for U.S. stocks would look like the past—that U.S. stocks would continue to provide great returns. That is the mistake I made. I forgot that important point. And history teaches us that events that never happened before can and do happen. If the events of September 11, 2001 taught you nothing else, they should have taught you that. The bottom line is that stocks are risky no matter the length of your investment horizon."

Hideki's advice was for Sammy to take no more equity risk than he had the ability, willingness and/or need to take. Sammy decided that it was good advice. After all, he had lost not only a large portion of his assets over the last three years, but he had also lost much sleep worrying. He decided that life was just too short to keep worrying. Since he could not be sure what the future would hold he would sell half of his stocks, take his losses, and return to his original 50/50 allocation. By selling now he would at least have Uncle Sam absorb some of the loss (the losses being tax deductible).

Sammy also admitted to himself that it was possible that stocks would recover. He was, therefore, giving up the upside potential that could be achieved with a 100 percent equity allocation. He was, however, unwilling to accept the downside risk that the U.S. markets would provide results similar to what Hideki had endured.

It is important to note that while the stock markets around the world did begin a strong recovery in 2003, believing that Sammy made the wrong decision to restore his original asset allocation is making the mistake of confusing strategy with outcome. In other words, an alternative universe might have shown up. If it had, Sammy would have experienced greater losses than he had the ability and willingness to accept.

The Moral of the Tale
The moral of the story is that stocks are risky no matter the length of your investment horizon. In fact, that is exactly why stocks have *generally* (but not always) provided such great returns over the long term. Investors know that stocks are always risky. Thus, they price stocks in a manner that provides them with an expected risk premium. In other words, stocks have to be priced low enough that they will attract investors with a risk premium that is large enough to compensate them for taking the risk of equity ownership. And because the majority of investors are risk averse, the equity risk premium has historically been large.

As an investor you should carefully evaluate your own unique ability, willingness and need to take risk, and never take more risk than is appropriate to your personal situation. This will help you avoid making the mistakes that were made by Sammy and Hideki.

You will also be well served if you remember these two important points. First, there is nothing new in investing, only the investment history you don't know (so know your history *before* you invest). Second, never treat the highly unlikely (a long, or even permanent, bear market) as impossible. As evidence of why this is so important, if we updated Hideki's story to January 2007, the Nikkei Index was still down almost 60 percent from the 40,000 level it had hit in 1989.

The next story addresses the conventional wisdom that the road to investment riches is to buy what you know.

One of the funny things about the stock market is that every time one man buys, another sells, and both think they are astute.

—William Feather

Chapter 11:
Buy What You Know

Steve, a salesman for a pharmaceutical firm, was also an amateur carpenter with an enviable workshop in his garage. He loved his hobby so much that he spent most of his weekends on home improvement projects, such as building kitchen cabinets and adding sky roofs. He just loved his Black & Decker tools. He felt that they were by far the best products on the market, and he knew his stuff. To take advantage of his knowledge he decided to make a large investment in the stock of this great company.

Being cautious by nature, before he bought the stock, he thought it prudent to do some research. He was pleased to find that Wall Street loved the stock as much as he loved the tools. The stock was even considered one of the "nifty-fifty"—a small group of "one-decision" stocks, companies so appealing it had been said that their stocks should always be bought and never sold, regardless of price.

Steve learned that Black & Decker was considered one of the greatest companies in the country, right up there with such leaders as IBM and Xerox. It was a leader in its field, with a strong balance sheet and high profit margins. In addition, earnings were expected to grow at double-digit rates. Steve felt that if ever there was a sure thing in the stock market, this was it.

With his insights confirmed, he bought the stock. The year was 1972. Unfortunately for Steve, the stock immediately headed south. However, Steve just knew that he was right. He also believed that if you just have patience, great companies will reward you in the end. Steve was patient. However, it was not until 1998 that Black & Decker finally recovered to the price he had paid twenty-six years earlier. Finally, having reached breakeven, Steve sold the stock. Looking back he discovered that during those twenty-six years the S&P 500 Index had returned almost 14 percent per annum.

A Fly in Your Soup

Martha was a housewife who also managed the family's finances. She loved researching stocks. She even belonged to an investment club. She focused her attention on companies whose products she used so that she could evaluate them herself. She certainly wasn't going to trust her family's finances to some stockbroker or security analyst.

Martha just loved the products made by Campbell's Soup. They were flavorful, convenient and the price was right. All of her friends bought Campbell's products. So Martha made a large investment in the stock. The year was 1961. Martha had to wait until 1982 for the stock to recover to the price she had paid. Finally having broken even, she decided to sell the stock. Looking back she discovered that over the same period the S&P 500 Index had returned about 8 percent per annum.

System Failure

Sally was a computer wizard. She worked in the technology department of a major securities firm. Her company had just made their single largest investment in technology ever. They were replacing all of their mainframes with mini-computers made by Digital Equipment. She was part of the team that made the recommendation. She was sure that these mini-computers were going to revolutionize the way data was processed. She decided to invest all of her savings in the stock. Before doing so, however, she thought it prudent to check with the security analyst who covered the stock at her firm. To her delight the analyst told her that Digital Equipment was the darling of Wall Street. It was one of the nifty-fifty. In fact, it was on the top of his buy list. That is all Sally needed to hear. She loaded up on the stock. The year was 1987. Within five years the stock had lost 85 percent of its value. She could not take the pain any longer and decided to sell.

A Waste of Energy

Sean was a senior executive with Enron. During his tenure the company had grown to become one of the top ten in the whole country in terms of the value of its stock. It had become the dominant player in the energy business in the United States. Its future looked even more promising. Both internal and external forecasts were for continued rapid growth in sales and earnings. Sean was happy that all of his 401(k) plan assets were invested in Enron stock. He was also looking at large gains from all the stock options he had exercised. He wasn't in the least bit worried about the margin loans (Enron stock was used as collateral) he had taken out in order to be able to exercise those options. He was sure that within five years he would be able to retire. The year was 1999. By the end of 2001, Enron had declared bankruptcy, and so had Sean. Retirement now looked a very long way off.

What Went Wrong?

The common thread through these four tales is that each of the investors did what conventional wisdom had taught them to do—buy what you know. Legendary investor Peter Lynch even wrote a book, *One Up On Wall Street: How To Use What You Already Know To Make Money In The Market*, extolling the virtues of such a strategy. So what went wrong?

Gary Belsky and Thomas Gilovich wrote a wonderful book, *Why Smart People Make Big Money Mistakes And How To Correct Them*. Among the many insights provided by the book is the following:

> "People overconfidently confuse familiarity with knowledge. For every example of a person who made money on an investment because she used a company's product or understood its strategy, we can give you five instances where such knowledge was insufficient to justify the investment."

Familiarity Breeds Investment

When AT&T was broken up, shareholders were given stock in each of what were called the Baby Bells. A study done a short while later found, however, that the residents of each region held a disproportionate number of shares of their local regional Bell. Each group of regional investors was confident that their regional Baby Bell would outperform the others. How else can you explain each investor having most of their eggs in one baby basket? This was not Lake Wobegon where all Baby Bells could outperform the average of the group.

Another example of familiarity breeding investment would be Georgia residents, who at the time of the study made up less than 3 percent of the U.S. population, owned 16 percent of all Coca-Cola stock. Why was this so? A logical explanation is that Coke has its headquarters in Atlanta. And why did people in Rochester, New York tend to own a disproportionate share of stock in Kodak and Xerox? The reason is that they both have large operations in Rochester.[1]

Clearly it is not any safer to own Coca-Cola if you live in Georgia than if you live in Rochester. And it is not any safer to own Kodak or Xerox if you live in Rochester than if you reside in Georgia (or anywhere else). Residents of Georgia got lucky in that Coca-Cola has provided fairly good returns. Residents of Rochester, on the other hand, had the other kind of luck. Should investment success depend upon where you reside?

Illusion of Safety

Familiarity breeds investment by creating an illusion of safety. Consider the following. It seems to be a global phenomenon that most investors hold the majority of their wealth in the form of domestic assets. Although the following data is a bit dated, it is unlikely that much has changed. In 1990, the domestic ownership shares of the world's five leading stock markets were the United States with 92 percent domestic stock ownership, Japan at 96 percent, United Kingdom 92 percent, Germany 79 percent and France 89 percent.[2] With the relative freedom of capital to travel around the world, the lack of global diversification cannot be explained by capital constraints. The only explanation is that investors in each country believe that their domestic market provides the best/safest investment opportunities. Investors in all five countries were taking the unnecessary risk of having almost all their eggs in a domestic basket, without any rational reason for doing so. It is simply a behavioral issue.

The Moral of the Tale

Investors are confronted with a major problem if they decide to buy individual stocks. The problem is that the universe from which they can choose is too large (there are about eight thousand U.S. stocks) for them to evaluate each company's merits. Note, however, that there is no such problem when deciding what to sell—unless you are willing to go short (bet that the stock will fall in price — not a wise decision given the potential for unlimited losses), your choices are limited to what you already own. And that is likely to be a relatively short list.

Investors solve the problem of which stocks to purchase (from the thousands available) by limiting their search to those companies with which they are most familiar. Perhaps they work for the company or use their products. But is that really a rational way to invest? Put simply, Peter Lynch was wrong—and so is the conventional wisdom. Buying a stock because you are familiar with the company or its products is not a rational way to make investment decisions. It not only confuses the familiar with the safe, but it also confuses information with knowledge—and that is the subject of our next tale.

Why do brokers exist? Why is there a whole industry devoted to helping individual investors pick out stocks when every jot of financial wisdom in the past fifty years, including Nobel prize-winning work, suggests that this is a mug's game?

—Holman Jenkins Jr. member of the editorial board of the *Wall Street Journal*

Chapter 12:
Why Did I Buy That Stock?

Harvey was a successful doctor who also considered himself to be a sophisticated investor. After a busy day at the office and hospital he would come home and head right for the computer. He had several favorite Web sites he liked to visit. He also read many periodicals and subscribed to several investment advisory newsletters. His portfolio consisted of about twenty individual stocks that he had thoroughly researched. And he only bought stocks whose business and products he understood well. Though he had never actually calculated the rate of return he had earned, he was confident that he had done well.

One day Harvey received a call from one of the stockbrokers with which he dealt. The broker was an employee of Merrill Lynch. After the usual pleasantries, the broker told Harvey "We just have to buy Merck." Now Harvey was no fool. He didn't just buy a stock because some broker told him to do so. So Harvey asked the broker "Why should I buy Merck?" The broker responded, "Our analyst covering Merck is a genius. She has a degree in molecular biology, graduated first in her class at Harvard, and received a Ph.D. from Duke, again graduating first in her class. Not only that, she worked for ten years at Merck in product development. Upon joining as our pharmaceuticals analyst, she has personally visited all of Merck plants and research facilities. She has also visited with Merck's competitors. Overall, she is confident that Merck has a tremendous pipeline of new products that will have little to no competition. The stock is currently selling at 45. Given her outlook for the new products and the growth in sales that will result, the stock is worth 100 if it's worth a penny." Harvey told the broker that the information sounded great, but that, as always, he wanted to do his own research. Harvey said he would call back tomorrow.

Confusing Information With Exploitable Knowledge
That night Harvey read all the research on Merck that was available on the Internet. Harvey was convinced that Merck was a great buy. The next day he called his broker and told him, "Thanks for the recommendation. I love it. Buy me 1,000 shares."

Whether the stock recommendation came from a fund manager, an investment advisor, or a friend, the story is surely a familiar one. There is a problem, however, with Harvey's reaction to the recommendation. The problem is that it is based on a false premise—that what the broker conveyed to him was not just information, but, instead, was knowledge that Harvey could use to identify a stock that somehow the market had mispriced. Being able to identify and then buy an undervalued stock, Harvey would be able to do what few individual and institutional investors have accomplished—outperform the market. Let's see why Harvey was operating under a false premise—why he was confusing information with knowledge that he could exploit.

Let's begin with the strong assumption that everything that Harvey was told by the Merrill Lynch broker was true (for example, there was a pipeline of great new products and sales and earnings were likely to grow rapidly). Even given this assumption, there is a logical reason that Harvey should have ignored the advice—and why you should ignore *all* such prognostications.

As the following explanation will make clear, the reason that you should ignore all such advice is that there is something wrong with the picture. Something the broker should have told Harvey, but never would—because if he did, Harvey would ignore the broker. It is just not in the broker's interest for Harvey to be an educated investor.

While Merrill Lynch probably does have a smart analyst covering Merck, there are probably more than fifty other smart analysts that also cover the company. It is also likely that most of them have degrees from top schools and have lots of experience. Almost certainly these analysts are all highly paid, motivated, and work diligently to gather all the facts. What Harvey, and the majority of investors fail to understand is that being smart and working hard to uncover information about a company is only a necessary condition for being able to outperform the market. The *sufficient* condition is that you have to either uncover information that others do not have (something that is difficult to do), and/or you have to be able to interpret that information better than does the collective wisdom of the entire market. And you have to do it in a way that compensates you for all of the expenses of the effort (and that should include not just the cost of trading but also placing value on the time it takes to perform the task). Listen carefully to these words of wisdom from Binkley Shorts, portfolio manager at Wellington Management: "When you're looking at companies like Microsoft, International Business Machines, Merck, and Coca-Cola, the ability to capture *incremental* insight is so damn challenging because so many people are looking at those stocks and it takes so long to get through the body of knowledge."[1] (Emphasis mine)

In the case of the recommendation to buy Merck, the other analysts covering the company almost certainly had the same information that the Merrill

Lynch broker had shared with Harvey. Given that they had the same information, and that they were likely to be just as smart, why was the stock not already trading at 100? Do you think all those smart people would let a stock that is obviously worth 100 sit there at 45 without rushing to buy it? The reason Merck is trading at 45 is that the market as a whole thinks that it is only worth 45, not 100. Louis Bachelier, a French economist, long ago remarked: "Clearly the price considered most likely by the market is the true current price: if the market judged otherwise, it would not quote this price, but another price higher or lower."[2]

What Harvey's broker should have told him is that his analyst thinks the rest of the world has got it wrong. What Harvey should have heard, because it was implicit in the broker's comments, is that "All the other smart analysts at Goldman Sachs and Morgan Stanley, etc. are wrong. They just don't get it. Only our analyst is *right*. The rest of the world is *wrong*. Only our analyst really knows this stuff, and the rest of those guys are simply misinterpreting the information." Now if Harvey had heard that explanation, being the smart person that he is, he would in all likelihood have hung up. Which is exactly what you should do the next time someone recommends a stock.

The Moral of the Tale
The next time you watch CNBC and listen to an analyst or fund manager tout even a hundred good reasons why to buy a specific stock, or equities in general, ignore the recommendation—even though you are likely to be impressed with the intellectual capacity of the person and the logic of the recommendation. In order to help you ignore seemingly sage advice, remember these two key insights about the information you just heard.

1. Capturing *incremental* insight is difficult, if not impossible, to achieve. The reason is that security analysts are competing with so many other smart and highly motivated people researching the same stocks. It is this tough competition that makes it so difficult to gain a competitive advantage. Imagine an art auction where you are the only expert among a group of amateurs. In that circumstance, it might be possible to find a bargain. On the other hand, if you are one of a group of mostly experts, it is less likely that you will find bargain prices. The same is true of stocks. Competition among all the professional active managers ensures that the market price is likely to be the correct price.

2. Think about where you just heard the new insightful information—*on*

national television. In the unlikely scenario this information was a secret, it certainly no longer is. The same analogy could be made for recommendations from any of the high-profile publications such as *Barron's, BusinessWeek, Fortune, Forbes, Money* or *Smart Money.*

Before concluding our tale, consider the following. At one time, there were about 35,000 investment clubs in America.[3] Thus, it is likely that there were nearly a half a million members. Each of these clubs was presumably researching companies hoping to identify stocks that would outperform the market. Armed with what you have now learned, ask yourself the following two questions:

1. Is it likely that a bunch of amateurs are going to be able to uncover information that the best and brightest professionals have failed to uncover?

2. Is it likely that the amateurs will be able to interpret the information better than the professionals?

I think it is safe to say that the odds that the answer is yes are slim or none. Yet those are the odds against which millions of investors are fighting—to the delight of brokers across the country. As the evidence presented in the tale of how markets set prices demonstrated, the members of investment clubs are playing a loser's game—a game they don't have to play.

In this light, consider the tale of the Beardstown Ladies. In the early 1990s, a group of women from Beardstown, Illinois, claimed to have found the formula to beat the market—what the majority of professional investors consistently fail to do. These women produced five investment books, including a best-seller. They became national icons. Yet no one thought to ask a few simple questions. As it turned out the Ladies never did outperform the market. They had made a mathematical error in calculating their returns (they counted their monthly dues, with which they bought stocks, as returns, not as principal invested). Once the error was uncovered, it was determined that they had actually underperformed the market by a wide margin. Could it be that the desire to beat the market runs so strong that investors throw away all wisdom and common sense?

The next story will reinforce the important moral of this tale.

Something that everyone knows isn't worth knowing.

—Bernard Baruch

Chapter 13:
Too Good to be True

Debbie was thrilled to hear that Harry Dent was coming to town to give a lecture at the local high school. Her reason: She worked for the U.S. Census Bureau and Harry Dent was a famous demographer. Dent was going to give a speech based on his book *The Roaring 2000s Investor: Strategies for the Life You Want*. Debbie was anxious to learn how she could use her knowledge of demographics to help her pick stocks that were sure to deliver great returns. After all, she knew that demographics is a science and Dent was highly regarded. She figured his books must be bestsellers for a good reason. And she had heard that millions of investors were now investing the "Harry Dent way." She wanted to get in on a good thing by learning how to apply her knowledge of demographics to the world of investing.

At the seminar Debbie listened carefully and took copious notes to make sure that she captured all of Harry Dent's insights. By the end of the talk, Debbie was so excited that she could hardly contain herself. Not only was Dent a great speaker, but he had also laid out a clear road map for investment success. Everything Dent said made great sense to her. The logic was impeccable.

Upon arriving home she organized her notes to make sure that she had clearly understood the major investment themes Dent introduced. She was able to narrow them down to the following:

- The population of the United States is rapidly aging.
- An aging population will boost the demand for certain products and services, benefiting those sectors (i.e., health care and pharmaceuticals).
- Individuals can benefit from these trends by investing in stocks of companies in those sectors of the economy.

While normally a cautious investor, Debbie decided that now was the time to be bold. The next day she would call her broker and place an order to buy the stocks of several of the leading pharmaceutical companies, as well as the stocks of a variety of companies that participated in the health care sector. She was so excited that she wanted to share what she had learned with Mona, her best friend.

Debbie told Mona about her plan. Fortunately for Debbie, Mona was skeptical of the plan. Something just didn't sound right.

Mona: Debbie, that all sounds logical, but it also sounds too easy. Before you rush to invest your life savings based on this strategy, let's think this through. I don't know much about the stock market, so help me out here. Debbie, tell me who does most of the trading in the stock market and, therefore, sets the prices of stocks?

Debbie: That is easy. It is not individual investors like you and me. Instead, it is the big institutional investors.

Mona: Who are they?

Debbie: They are pension plans, mutual funds and hedge funds.

Mona: Are the people who make the investment decisions on behalf of those institutions intelligent?

Debbie: Of course they are. They know what they are doing or they would not be managing billions of dollars.

Mona: That makes sense to me. Now do you think it is likely that even a single one of these smart institutional fund managers is unaware that the population of the United States is getting older?

Debbie: Of course not.

Mona: Okay. Now let's take that one step further. Since they know that the population is aging, do you think that it is possible that these smart investors are unaware that since the population is aging, that the demand for health care is going to rise rapidly?

Debbie: Of course not.

Mona: And if the demand for health care is going to rise rapidly, do you think that these same smart investors are unable to figure out that the profits of companies in the health care sector are likely to rise rapidly?

Debbie: Of course not. They know it. But what is your point?

Mona: My point is this: If they know this, isn't it logical to believe that the prices of the stocks of the companies you are ready to rush out and buy already reflect those great expectations?

Debbie: I guess so.

Mona: And if the companies are so likely to achieve great earnings, doesn't that make them safe investments?

Debbie: Sure, but that is the point. I can get great returns without taking lots of risk.

Mona: Debbie, that cannot be. I don't know much about investing, but I have always heard that risk and expected return are related. And thus if these are as safe investments as you say they are, and the current prices reflect great expectations, how can you expect to get high returns? Don't you have to take lots of risk if you want to earn high returns?

Debbie was deflated. Mona's line of thinking made so much sense that she was embarrassed that she had not thought of it herself. How could she have been so wrong? She thanked Mona for her insights and decided to sleep on it. First thing in the morning she ran out to get a copy of the *Wall Street Journal*. She immediately opened up the paper to the section that showed the closing stock prices of the prior day. She wanted to see how the market was pricing some of the companies in which she had planned to invest *relative* to how the rest of the stocks were priced. She first noted that the price-to-earnings (P/E) ratio of the S&P 500 was a bit less than nineteen.

The first stock on Debbie's list was Pfizer, the leading pharmaceuticals company. She was disappointed to learn that it was trading at a P/E of thirty, almost 60 percent more expensive than the market. She then checked the price of the other pharmaceutical company she had planned to buy, Eli Lilly & Company. She found that its P/E ratio was over twenty-six, about 40 percent richer than the market. Next on the list was Roche Holding, a large international pharmaceutical company. She found that it was trading at a P/E of over thirty-six, almost double that of the market. This was getting discouraging. It sure looked like Mona was right. She decided to check the price of one more stock, Genentech, the leading biotechnology company. It was trading at a P/E of seventy, 268 percent richer than the market. That was enough. She called Mona to tell her what she had found and to thank her for preventing a terrible mistake.

The Moral of the Tale

What Debbie learned was that Harry Dent had made the mistake of confusing information with knowledge that you could use to generate above market returns. A rapidly growing population, leading to rapid growth in demand for health care products and services, and, in turn, a rapid growth in profits for providers of such products and services was nothing more than information. It conveyed no knowledge that she could use.

There is another lesson that Debbie needed to learn about trying to benefit from such obvious trends. Mona could have also told Debbie that even if she knew with 100 percent certainty that the demand for a certain product or service would rapidly rise, that information tells her little, if anything, about future profits in the industry.

For example, certainly the demand for cell phones continued to rise at a rapid pace from 2000 through 2006. Despite the rapid rise in demand, investors who were able to correctly forecast this trend would have experienced losses had they invested in stocks of providers (e.g., Nokia) of this product. The reason is that the supply exceeded demand and prices for their products and services fell, taking stock prices with them.

The next tale discusses one of the most common investor mistakes, having too many eggs in one basket.

Diversification for investors, like celibacy for teenagers, is a concept both easy to understand and hard to practice.

—James Gipson, former manager of the Clipper Fund

Chapter 14:
Too Many Eggs in One Basket

Jay was recently promoted to Chief Executive Officer of a Fortune 500 company. He was pleased to hear that along with a significant salary increase and a large increase in stock options, he received some new benefits. Among them, access to the services of a highly regarded financial planner, Robert Smith.

While knowing that he needed to focus on issues related to estate and tax planning, retirement planning, insurance, etc., Jay had always procrastinated. The availability of this benefit was just the impetus he needed to help him focus on these issues. He had heard great things about Robert from some of his friends. He decided to call him and set up a meeting. Robert requested that Jay send him copies of all of his financial statements, wills, etc. to make the meeting as productive as possible.

After the usual pleasantries, Robert told Jay that while there were some estate planning issues that needed to be addressed, in general, his affairs were in good shape. There was, however, one major problem that he wanted to discuss. The conversation went as follows:

Robert: Your investable net worth is $4 million. Invested prudently you should not have any problem achieving your financial objectives and living a comfortable lifestyle without the need to take a great deal of risk. The problem is that 75 percent, or $3 million, of your financial assets are concentrated in your company's stock.

Jay: I don't see that as a problem. My company is the dominant player in our industry, we have a strong balance sheet and the earnings outlook is great.

Robert: I am glad you work for such a great company. I am sure that you don't want to sell the stock you hold because you are convinced that it is going to outperform the market. Is that correct?

Jay: Exactly.

Robert: I understand why you would think that you are doing the right thing by holding onto all those shares. Ultimately all decisions are yours. You have to live with the results and consequences of the outcomes. I view my role as one of an educator. It is my objective to make sure you make informed decisions. In order to do that, I have to be sure that you understand the nature of the risks you take and the pros and cons of any strategy. So I ask that you keep an open mind as we discuss this important issue.

Jay: I like to think that I always keep an open mind.

Robert: Almost every day I meet executives with similar tales. Let me tell you about a few of them. Last week I met with an executive from IBM. His net worth was $7 million, and $5 million of that was in IBM stock. I asked him why he had so many eggs in one basket. His answer was similar to yours. He too was confident that the stock was going to outperform the market. Then I met with an executive from Citicorp whose net worth was $5 million, of which $3 million was in Citicorp stock. He too was confident that the stock was going to outperform the market. And then I met with an executive from General Electric. He was just as confident about the stock's outlook as were the others. And I could tell you hundreds of similar tales. Now Jay, is it possible that all of these bright and successful executives can be right? Can all of their stocks outperform the market? Obviously, it is not possible that they can all beat the market. The reason is that collectively they are the market. While each executive is equally confident about the likely success of his company, some will turn out to have been overconfident, and thus wrong. And the cost of being wrong can be great if you have almost all of your eggs in one basket.

Jay, I have found it useful in situations like yours to have you consider how you would react if you were a player in a real-life game of chance. It is important that you treat this seriously. Here is how the game works. I am going to roll a die. If the die comes up one, two, three, four, or five, you win. If the die comes up six you lose. Your net investable net worth is $4 million. I am going to allow you to bet any amount you choose, from zero to a maximum of $4 million. However, we are only going to roll the die once. I should add that your wife and three lovely daughters will be standing next to you as you decide how much to bet. Now I think we can agree that this is the best bet you will ever have the opportunity to make. The odds are 5:1 in your favor. Before considering how much you want to bet, keep in mind that while the odds are favorable, if many people play the game we would expect that one in every six would lose. With the knowledge that the unlikely is possible (a six appearing and you lose), how much of your $4 million are you willing to bet?

Jay: I think I would bet about $10,000.

Robert: That is a typical answer. The majority of answers fall in the range of 0 to 10 percent. Rarely do I hear an answer of more than 25 percent. I want to point out that there is no right answer to the question—just an answer that is right for you based on your own unique ability, willingness and need to take risk. There is an important point to take away from this example. When the odds of winning are great, but the cost of losing is high, we tend to become risk averse. And the greater the cost of losing, the more risk averse we become.

The reason is that we are usually smart enough to not treat even the highly unlikely as impossible. Although I know the answers to the following questions, to illustrate this point I need to ask them. Do you buy homeowners insurance?

Jay: Yes.

Robert: Do you expect the house will burn down or be struck by lightning?

Jay: No.

Robert: In fact, you know that the odds of collecting on your policy are low. Thus, by purchasing insurance you are likely to end up transferring dollars from your pocket to the pocket of the insurance company. Do you have a life insurance policy?

Jay: Yes.

Robert: Do you know that the odds of someone your age and in your health condition dying in the next year are about 100:1? Since I know you don't expect to die in the near future, why are you almost certainly transferring assets from your family to the insurance company?

Jay: Because while it is not likely I will die prematurely, it is possible.

Robert: That is exactly the point I want to convey. When the cost of being wrong is great, even when something is highly unlikely, you choose to avoid the risk—except when it comes to your company's stock! In the cases of life and homeowners insurance the odds of a major loss are far lower than the odds of your stock underperforming the market. Yet you chose to avoid those risks, but accept the risk on your stock. And in the dice game when you had odds of 5:1 in your favor, you choose to bet only a small amount. Now I know that even after the stories I have told you might still be confident that your company's stock will outperform the market. I hope that you would agree, however, that the odds that it will do so are not greater than 5:1 (the odds in your favor in the dice game) that it will outperform the market.

Jay, every investor knows intuitively that putting too many eggs in one basket is a risky investment decision that can easily be avoided by building a diversified portfolio. Yet many executives, and long-term corporate employees end up with a substantial portion of their assets in the stock of their employer. Familiarity with their employer causes them to be overconfident. They are making the mistake of confusing something that is familiar with something that is safe. What they are failing to consider is that while individual stocks do offer the possibility of market-beating returns, they also create the possibility of disastrous results. The risk of a complete loss is highest when holding an individual stock, but is significantly minimized when holding a diversified portfolio. Diversification is like buying insurance in that you minimize the risk of a disastrous outcome.

There is another important point I want to make regarding the risks you are taking. Let me ask you this question. If your company does well, are you likely do well, even if you didn't own as much stock as you do now?

Jay: Sure, my salary would increase. I would get big bonuses. I would get more stock options. And my existing options would become highly profitable.

Robert: Now consider the other possibility. What would happen if the company did poorly?

Jay: My compensation would suffer.

Robert: And is it possible that you might even get fired?

Jay: I guess so.

Robert: And what would happen to the value of your stock and all those options?

Jay: The stock price would suffer and my options might even become worthless.

Robert: In effect by continuing to own lots of stock in the same company from which you receive your paycheck you are playing a game of double jeopardy—you are at risk on your source of income and you are also at risk on the value of your investments. That doesn't seem to be a prudent thing to do if the cost of being wrong can be great—which in your case, you have to admit, it is.

I want to make sure that you don't make the same mistake executives at such once high flyers as Enron and MCI made. They watched almost all of their net worth evaporate because they made the mistakes of confusing the familiar with the safe and treating the highly unlikely as impossible.

I would like to give you one more example to demonstrate why you should neither be overconfident, nor treat the highly unlikely as impossible. If ever there was a safe stock, it was Pacific Gas & Electric (PG&E). This California utility was what is often referred to as a "widows and orphans" stock—it was so safe that even widows and orphans could own it. That is what many PG&E employees thought. It is quite common for employees to have a large percentage of their 401(k) or profit sharing plans invested in the stock of their company (though sometimes not by their choice). And this was likely the case at PG&E. Unfortunately, as a result of the California energy crisis the company declared bankruptcy in the first quarter of 2001. Many long-time employees, some on the verge of retiring, suffered devastating losses—losses from which they could never recover.

Hopefully, I have convinced you that holding 75 percent of your assets in the stock of any one company—let alone that of your employer—is too risky.

The upside gain that might be achieved is not worth the risk of the substantial pain that would be suffered if the wrong outcome were to occur. And, more importantly, given the level of wealth you have achieved, there is no need to take such concentrated risk. You can achieve your financial goals while at the same time substantially reducing your risk by diversifying not only across the various equity asset classes, but also by moving a significant portion of your holdings into much safer bonds.

Jay: I get the message.

Robert: Great. Now I would like you to consider the following situation. Let's imagine that your net worth was just $1 million and none of it was invested in your company's stock. You learn that you have just inherited $3 million. How much, if any, of the $3 million would you invest in your company's stock?

Jay: I see the point. I would not invest anywhere near $3 million. Perhaps I would invest 10 percent of the amount—though now even that sounds like a large figure. I bet I can guess your next question. If I would not buy more than 10 percent, why am I holding 75 percent?

Robert: You got it. Every day you make the decision to hold the stock, you are making the decision to buy it. The reason is that you don't have to continue to own it. Instead, you can sell it.

Jay: You have convinced me of the logic. If I sell my stock, however, I will have to pay a large capital gains tax since my cost basis is very low.

Robert: Let me explain something I learned a long time ago: There is only one thing worse than having to pay taxes. Do you know what that is?

Jay: No, but I am sure you are going to tell me.

Robert: *Not* having to pay them. Consider the following story. It happened to a friend of mine. Having worked at Intel for a long time, and being a senior executive, he had accumulated lots of stock. With the stock trading at over seventy, his holdings were worth about $10 million dollars. I gave him the same advice I have given you—SELL. Despite the logic of the arguments I made (and he agreed with every one of them), for a variety of reasons he could not get himself to sell. First, he was very confident the company would continue to prosper. Second, if he sold it would show a lack of faith in the company's future and he thought he would feel like a traitor. Third, his cost basis was very low and he did not want to pay the tax.

He watched the stock drop to sixty, then fifty, then forty, and then to thirty. Finally, he told me that if the stock would just get back to forty he would sell. I reminded him that just because it had once been forty doesn't mean it has to go back there again.

Investors in once great companies such as Polaroid and Xerox are still waiting, decades later, for their stocks to return to levels they had previously attained. Well it is now several years later. My friend suffered as the stock dropped below twenty, recovered to about thirty, and then fell sharply again. He is still holding his shares. Unfortunately, they are now worth about $3 million. And while he won't suffer in retirement, he can no longer afford the luxuries he might have enjoyed had he taken the prudent course.

The bottom line is that while trying to minimize taxes is a worthy objective, that objective should never be allowed to override a prudent risk management strategy. In addition, you are lucky in your timing. The capital gains tax is currently the lowest it has been in more than 70 years. I could cite many examples of stocks that have dropped that much in just one day. In fact, in December 2006 that is exactly what happened to Pfizer after a poor earnings announcement. Imagine how you would feel if you were one of the executives at Pfizer who had decided not to sell the company stock because they did not want to pay the tax. In their case they would have been better off selling even if the cost basis had been zero.

There is one other point to consider. I noted in your tax returns that you give a substantial amount every year to various charities. Instead of giving cash, as you have in the past, you can donate your appreciated shares and take a deduction for their full market value. In that way you will avoid paying any tax. We could even set up a charitable trust. We could then put some of the shares into the trust, sell them off, and diversify the risk. That would allow you to take a tax deduction today, while distributing the assets to various charities over time.

Jay: That sounds like a great idea. Let's get together next week and develop a plan to sell off a significant portion of the stock and diversify the portfolio. This has been a great meeting. I really learned a lot. Thanks for helping me.

Robert: It's been my pleasure.

The Moral of the Tale

Having more than a relatively small amount (perhaps up to 10 percent) of your investable net worth in any one stock moves you away from being an investor toward being a speculator—not a prudent decision when substantial dollars are involved. Thus, concentrated positions should be avoided whenever possible. Ron Ross, author of *The Unbeatable Market*, put it this way: "The safest port in a sea of uncertainty is diversification."[1]

Portfolio risk can be substantially reduced by selling the concentrated position and using the proceeds to build a globally diversified portfolio that reflects your unique ability, willingness and need to take risk. Finally, if you are ever tempted to put lots of eggs in one basket, remember that while this is the surest way to *make* a fortune, it is also the surest way to *lose* one.

The next tale addresses the conventional wisdom that if a strategy isn't working you need to change it.

Individual decisions can be badly thought through, and yet be successful, or exceedingly well thought through, but be unsuccessful, because the recognized possibility of failure in fact occurs. But over time, more thoughtful decision-making will lead to better results, and more thoughtful decision-making can be encouraged by evaluating decisions on how well they were made rather than on outcome.

—Robert Rubin, Harvard Commencement Address, 2001 (Michael J. Mauboussin, *More Than You Know*, p. 9. Columbia University Press, 2006)

Chapter 15:
Confusing Before-the-Fact Strategy and After-the-Fact Outcome

Mark and Larry were brothers who ran a family business. In late 1994 they sold the business and each received $6 million after taxes. While they were smart businessmen, neither had much experience or knowledge about investing. Until this point, almost all of their assets had been tied up in the family business. Since the proceeds from the sale of the business represented the "nest egg" on which they were going to retire, they wanted to be sure that it would be managed well. Both in their forties, Mark and Larry knew this nest egg was going to have to last a long time.

After interviewing several investment advisors they decided to work with Jason Scott. Jason had impressed them with his investment approach. While the other advisors they had met all touted their ability to beat the market, Jason's approach was grounded in academic theory that made sense when he explained it. And unlike the other advisors, he was able to back up his claims with solid evidence.

Jason explained that his approach was based on three fundamental beliefs. First, building a globally diversified portfolio reduced the risk of having too many eggs in one basket. Their portfolios would contain mutual funds that would provide exposure to a prudent mix of both domestic and international equities. It would include small and large stocks, value and growth stocks, and real estate. They would each also have an appropriate amount of bonds to reduce the risk of an all-equity portfolio. Second, efforts to outperform the market were unlikely to produce market-beating returns. Therefore, trying to minimize costs is more important than trying to outperform the market. Thus, the funds they would own would be low-cost, no-load and passively managed funds. Third, it was important to be a disciplined, long-term, buy-and-hold investor.

Jason showed them the historical evidence that over the long term a globally diversified portfolio had produced superior returns relative to the returns earned on what investors typically hold—a mostly, or even all, U.S. large-cap portfolio. And it had done so with less volatility. Jason was careful to also point out that while the more diversified portfolio had produced superior returns over the long term, it did not do so every year. And while the evidence and logic suggests that it would continue to produce superior risk-adjusted returns, there was no guarantee that it would. That was the nature of risk. You have to decide on the right strategy without knowing what will be the outcome. The key to success, he stressed, was to be a disciplined, long-term investor.

Both Mark and Larry agreed that Jason was the preferred choice. They both became clients of Jason's at the end of the year. While Mark and Larry each maintained their own accounts they had independently decided on the same exact portfolio.

Their first year working with Jason was, in some respects, a pretty good year. Their equity portfolio was up over 25 percent. Most of their friends had, however, done even better. The S&P 500 Index was up over 37 percent. While expressing disappointment to both Jason and each other, they recognized that it was just one year.

The next year, 1996, produced similar results. Their equity holdings again produced better than expected results, rising over 16 percent. Unfortunately, many of their friends did better as the S&P 500 Index rose over 23 percent. Again, they told Jason that while the returns were good in an absolute sense, they were poor in a relative sense. Jason reminded them that it was only two years and that they had committed to being long-term, disciplined investors. They once again agreed to be patient.

The next year, 1997, produced similar, but even more disappointing results. While their equity portfolio again produced a return of about 17 percent, the S&P 500 Index almost doubled that figure. Now it was three years in a row of underperformance. They were actually getting concerned and raised the issue with Jason. He reminded them that he had told them that even longer periods of relative underperformance were possible. He also asked them if they no longer believed that diversification was the prudent strategy. Though getting nervous that they may have made the wrong decision, they agreed once again to stay the course.

Unfortunately, 1998 brought the worst year yet. While the S&P 500 Index was up over 28 percent, their equities had risen less than 7 percent. At their annual meeting they again expressed their concern. Jason told them that nothing had changed and that there was no evidence or logic that convinced him that there was a more prudent investment strategy than the one they had already adopted. They told Jason that they would give it one more year.

While 1999 produced relatively better results, for the fifth year in a row the diversified portfolio, having risen 18 percent, had underperformed the

106

S&P 500 Index by 3 percent. Mark and Larry were extremely disappointed. They told Jason that they had decided to leave. What really convinced them was that they had calculated that every $1 they had invested in equities with Jason had grown to not much more than $2. If they had instead invested the same $1 in the S&P 500 Index it would have grown to about $3.50. Jason acknowledged that those figures were correct. He asked only that before they made that decision final, he wanted to ask them a few questions.

Jason: Mark and Larry, I know you are both married and have kids. I assume both of you have life insurance?

Mark: Sure we do.

Jason: How long have you been paying premiums on that insurance?

Mark: In my case about ten years and in Larry's about twenty.

Jason: Do you know what the odds are that a healthy male your age, who neither smokes nor drinks excessively, will die in the next year? I can tell you that they are extremely low. Yet you both have kept buying insurance all these years with the almost certain knowledge that all you were likely doing was transferring assets from your accounts to the life insurance company's accounts. Now why would you do a foolish thing like that?

Larry: Because while it was unlikely that I would die, it was not impossible, and the cost of being wrong is too great.

Jason: Does either of you, even in hindsight, believe that it was a bad decision to have bought that life insurance?

Mark: No, of course not.

Jason: So then you agree that in a world where you cannot foresee the future we should never judge the correctness of a strategy by the resulting outcome. In other words, we should only judge the correctness of a strategy before we know the outcome, not afterwards. Either the strategy is correct before the fact, or it is wrong before the fact. If you disagree, then you have to say that buying the insurance was a bad decision since neither of you has collected on it lately. Do you agree?

Mark and Larry: Yes.

Jason: Well, diversification is like insurance. The strategy of buying insurance is working whether you collect on the policy or not. And I hope that it is a long time before either of your policies pays off. In the case of the strategy of diversification, it too is always working. It is just that sometimes you like the results and sometimes you don't. When you don't like the results, it doesn't mean the decision was wrong any more than it does in the life insurance example I just gave you.

Mark and Larry, I would like you to recall our initial meeting five years ago. At that time I showed you the long-term historical evidence that a diversified portfolio produced superior risk-adjusted returns. And you agreed with the logic. I also told you that it was quite possible, if not even likely, that we would experience periods, potentially long ones, of underperformance. And I told you that the key to being a successful investor was to have the discipline to stay the course. As Benjamin Disraeli stated: "Patience is a necessary ingredient of genius." Nothing has changed. And I don't think you should change your strategy.

Jason concluded by suggesting that they think over what he had told them and he would call them next week to follow up. They agreed to think it over. The following week Jason called Larry first. Larry told him that while he was disappointed in the results, he was swayed by the logic of Jason's arguments. He was going to stay the course. Jason thanked him for his confidence.

Jason called Mark next. Mark told him that after thinking it over and speaking with several friends he had decided to make a change. He was going to switch to another advisor that invested in the "new economy." He told Jason that while everything he had told them had made sense at the time, he was now convinced that this time it was different. We were living in a new era where the old rules didn't apply.

Jason told Mark that he was disappointed but that he also understood. He told Mark that he would make the transfer of funds as quickly as possible. He also told Mark that he would keep his accounts open and continue to report the results as if Mark had remained a client. In that way Mark would be able to compare the results of his new strategy to those of the strategy that he had just abandoned.

In 2000, the diversified portfolio returned about 1 percent, while the S&P 500 Index lost about 9 percent. In 2001, while the diversified portfolio returned about 4 percent, the S&P 500 Index lost about 12 percent. In 2002, the diversified portfolio lost almost 11 percent, while the S&P 500 Index lost more than twice as much. And in 2003, while the diversified portfolio returned almost 50 percent, the S&P 500 Index rose just 29 percent.

Larry, of course, was thrilled that he was rewarded for staying the course. Mark, on the other hand, was another story. He deliberated as to whether he should swallow his pride and admit he was wrong. He knew that Jason would be happy to have him back as a client and that Jason had even kept his accounts open.

What eventually convinced Mark to return? Larry shared the following calculation with him. For the four years after Mark abandoned the strategy the diversified portfolio had produced a cumulative return of almost 40 percent.

On the other hand the S&P 500 Index had lost 20 percent. Larry also showed him that over the entire nine-year period every dollar Larry had invested had now grown to just over $3, while every dollar invested in the S&P 500 Index was now worth just $2.80 cents.

To make matters worse, Larry showed Mark that Jason was also right that being a disciplined long-term investor was one of the keys to success. Because Mark had switched strategies, beginning with the diversified portfolio in 1995 and then switching to the S&P portfolio in 2000, every dollar he invested had grown to just $1.71. Mark would have been better off with either strategy; a diversified or a more concentrated one. The worst result came from switching strategies. Instead of staying the course, Mark had effectively bought high and sold low. Seeing that figure convinced Mark that his financial future was more important than his pride. Larry consoled Mark and reminded him that while even smart people make mistakes, only fools repeat them. Mark called Jason the very next day and once again became a client——this time for life.

The Moral of the Tale

"Investors often make the critical mistake of assuming that good outcomes are the result of a good process and bad outcomes imply a bad process."[1] As hedge fund manager and author Nassim Nicholas Taleb pointed out: "One cannot judge a performance in any given field (war, politics, medicine, investments) by the results, but by the costs of the alternative (if history played out in a different way). Such substitute courses of events are called alternative histories. Clearly, the quality of a decision cannot be solely judged based on its outcome, but such a point seems to be voiced only by people who fail (those who succeed attribute their success to the quality of their decision)."[2] Thus, the moral of our story is that a strategy can only be judged to be a good or a poor one before we know the outcome. Those who do otherwise are often making the mistake of confusing skill and luck.

The next story discusses how investors are often their own worst enemies.

The investor's chief problem—and even his worst enemy—is likely to be himself.

—Benjamin Graham

Chapter 16:
An Investor's Worst Enemy

Like most boys growing up in New York City I spent much of my childhood and teenage years with a basketball pretty much glued to my hand. I was a fairly good athlete and even managed to make my college's basketball team as a freshman. Now that is not saying much. Baruch College was a Division III school and I mostly sat at the end of the bench. By the end of the season I probably had accumulated more splinters than minutes played. I also played lots of baseball, softball and football. Unfortunately, since there were not many tennis courts in the Bronx, I did not get to play often.

At the age of twenty-five I moved to San Francisco. Everyone there played tennis. So I became a tennis player. After a relatively short time, because of my athletic skills, I became what you might call a decent weekend player. However, I was often frustrated by the fact that there were players that consistently beat me despite the fact that I was the better athlete. It was particularly frustrating when I lost to a player that was decades older. Eventually, after about twenty years, I finally figured out that while I was a better athlete, they were better tennis players—and there is a big difference between the two.

With this "revelation," I finally decided to attend a tennis clinic. At the end of the week each of the participants got to play for an hour with the tennis pro. During my session with the pro I learned something that dramatically improved my tennis game. It also provided me with an insight about games in general.

Like most weekend players my weaker shot was the backhand. During a rally the tennis pro hit a shot deep into my backhand corner. He then came to the net, putting even more pressure on me. Amazingly, I hit a great passing shot that landed deep in the court and just inside the line. After making that shot the pro called me to the net. I was sure he was going to compliment me. Instead, what he said was "That shot will be your worst enemy." He explained that while it was an exceptional shot, it was not a high-percentage one for a good "weekend player" like me. Remembering how good that shot felt, I would try to repeat it. Unfortunately, I would be successful on an infrequent basis. He pointed out that while he could make that shot perhaps 90 percent of the time, I was likely to make it less than 10 percent of the time. The pro then asked me if I wanted to make great shots or would I rather win matches? Up until that point I thought that one was the cause of the other. The pro taught me otherwise.

The pro explained that in the game played by weekend warriors such as myself, most points are not *won* by hitting shots that cannot be returned by the opponent. Instead, the majority of points are *lost* when balls are hit into the net, long or outside the lines in a failed attempt to hit those exceptional winning shots. That is why this type of strategy produces what is called a loser's game. The pro was also polite enough to say that it is not the *people* who play the game who are losers; instead it is the *strategy* they are following that is a losing one.

To improve my results, the pro told me that in order to find the winning strategy I had to understand the type of game I was playing. Since, unlike professional tennis players, I am certainly not capable of consistently hitting winning shots, I was playing a loser's game. Instead of trying to hit winners (and likely hitting the ball long, wide or into the net), I should just try to hit the ball safely back, with a bit of pace, and use the middle of the court. Let the opponent play the loser's game. Recognizing the brilliance of his insight, I immediately put his advice to work with astonishingly good results. I was now regularly beating players with whom I had previously experienced difficulty.

What does tennis have to do with investing? Simply this: Consistently successful investing requires a successful strategy. The majority of individual investors (and most professionals) try to beat the market. They do so by attempting to uncover individual securities they believe the rest of the market has somehow mispriced (the price is too high or too low). They also try to time their investment decisions so that they are buying when the market is "undervalued" and selling when it is "overvalued." Such a strategy is known as active portfolio management. Occasionally, with the same infrequent timing of my great tennis shots, these active portfolio managers will make the proverbial killing. On the other hand, over the long run, the likelihood is that they will lose (underperform) more often than they will win (outperform). Thus, the evidence demonstrates that while the winning strategy in tennis is different for professionals and amateurs, the winning strategy is the same for all investors, whether they are individuals or institutions.

In loser's tennis, the winning strategy is not to play the loser's game. The same is true in the "game" of investing. The winning strategy is not to play— just accept market returns by investing in passively managed funds.

You have already seen the evidence on the failure of even the very best professionals (in the story When Even the Best Are Not Likely to Win)—the majority of professional investors succeed at beating simple passive benchmarks about as often as I was able to hit a shot that the teaching pro was unable to return (it was the only point I won that day). The reason they fail is that they are trying to hit that great shot (finding mispriced securities) instead of just getting the ball back (simply accepting market returns). If the top active managers in the world fail with such regularity, what are the odds that you will succeed?

In the face of such overwhelming evidence, the puzzling question is why do people keep trying to play a game they are likely to lose? From my perspective, there are four explanations. One explanation is that because our education system has failed investors (and Wall Street and most of the financial media want to conceal the evidence) they are unaware of the evidence. A second explanation is that while the evidence suggests playing the game of active management is the triumph of hope over wisdom and experience, hope does spring eternal—after all a small minority do succeed. A third explanation is that active management is exciting, while passive management is boring. A fourth explanation is that investors are overconfident—a normal human condition, one not limited to investing. While each investor might admit that it is hard to beat the market, each believes that somehow he will be one of the few that will succeed.

University of Chicago professor Richard Thaler and Yale professor Robert J. Shiller noted that "individual investors and money managers persist in their beliefs that they are endowed with more and better information than others, and that they can profit by picking stocks."[1] Ninety percent think they're above average. This insight helps explain why individual investors believe they can pick stocks that will outperform the market, time the market and identify the few active managers who will beat their respective benchmarks. Gus Sauter, who manages a wide array of index funds for Vanguard and one actively managed fund, provided this insight: "Like everybody else in this industry I have an ego large enough to believe I'm going to be one of the select few that will outperform."[2]

Perhaps the most amusing example of overconfidence might be the results of the Mensa investment club—though it could not have been amusing to them—as their results make the Beardstown Ladies look like Warren Buffett. Mensa is a club that limits its membership to those individuals that are in the top 2 percent as measured by I.Q. If anyone has a right to be confident that their intellectual capacity would allow them to achieve superior investment results it would seem that it should be the members of Mensa.

The June 2001 issue of *Smart Money* reported that over the prior fifteen years the Mensa investment club returned just 2.5 percent, underperforming the S&P 500 Index by almost 13 percent per annum. Warren Smith, an investor for thirty-five years, reported that his original investment of $5,300 had turned into $9,300. A similar investment in the S&P 500 Index would have produced almost $300,000. One investor described their strategy as buy low, sell lower. The Mensa members were overconfident that their superior intellectual skills could be translated into superior investment returns. Overconfidence can be very expensive.

The example of the Mensa investment club proves the wisdom of Peter Bernstein's insight: "The essence of investment theory is that being smart is not a *sufficient* condition for being rich."[3] (Emphasis mine) As mentioned earlier, one objective of this book is to provide you with the missing ingredients (the necessary conditions for investment success).

Investors would be wise to listen to *Wall Street Journal* columnist Jonathan Clements who made the following observation: "Beat the market? The idea is ludicrous. Since very few investors manage to beat the market, but in an astonishing triumph of hope over experience millions of investors keep trying."[4] Overconfidence provides the explanation for this behavior. Investors may even recognize the difficulty of the task; yet they still believe that they can succeed with a high degree of probability. As author and personal finance journalist James Smalhout put it, "Psychologists have long documented the tendency of *Homo sapiens* to overrate his own abilities and prospects for success. This is particularly true of the subspecies that invests in stocks and, accordingly, tends to overtrade."[5]

Gary Belsky and Thomas Gilovich, authors of the wonderful book, *Why Smart People Make Big Money Mistakes*, reached the following conclusion:

> "Any individual who is not professionally occupied in the financial services industry (and even most of those who are) and who in any way attempts to actively manage an investment portfolio is probably suffering from overconfidence. That is, anyone who has confidence enough in his or her abilities and knowledge to invest in a particular stock or bond (or actively managed mutual fund or real estate investment trust or limited partnership) is most likely fooling himself. In fact, most such people—probably you—have no business at all trying to pick investments, except perhaps as sport. Such people—again, probably you—should simply divide their money among several index mutual funds and turn off CNBC."[6]

Having been presented with several tales that provide the logic and evidence on why passive investing is the winner's game, hopefully, you will allow wisdom and experience to triumph over hope and overconfidence. If, however, you are still undecided, consider the following. It is estimated that the revenues of the institutions that make their living from the capital market exceeds $150 billion per year. This is the portion of the returns that the markets provide that is *removed* (from your pockets) by financial intermediaries. That amount might approach as much as 2 percent per annum of the total stock and bond markets![7] Consider these words of wisdom from author Ron Ross: "The people on Wall Street simply can't imagine how they would make a living if they weren't trying to beat the market. But that's their problem, not yours. It's not your responsibility to provide livelihoods for stock analysts. What's rational on Wall Street isn't usually aligned with the best interests of you as an investor."[8]

The Moral of the Tale
To echo the sentiments of *Wall Street Journal* columnist Jonathan Clements: If you want to see the greatest threat to your financial future, go home and take a look in the mirror.[9] If you decide to play the loser's game of active investing the only people you will likely be enriching are your broker, the manager of the actively managed mutual fund or portfolio in which you are investing, and the publisher of the newsletter, magazine, or ratings service to which you are subscribing.

The next story addresses the issue of what defines prudent investing.

115

There is one thing stronger than all the armies of the world, and that is an idea whose time has come.

—Victor Hugo

Chapter 17:
A Higher Intelligence

For many years, a group of higher beings had monitored the advancement of society on Earth through sound waves that reached their distant planet. Although the beings agreed that Earth's civilization had generally progressed over the last millennium, they had become interested in certain communications emitting from the United States. Specifically, communications regarding investment propaganda—seemingly popular theories espousing that the way to prudently invest was to pick stocks and time the market. They wondered why investors would believe such foolish theories when the evidence from their own experiences clearly demonstrated that those benefiting from such strategies were the purveyors of these theories (brokers, investment bankers, mutual fund sponsors and especially hedge fund managers). Still, the beings assumed that U.S. investors would eventually realize the errors of their ways and abandon the prevailing investment theories.

Watching investors continue to subscribe to such investment strategies (often with disastrous results) eventually compelled the beings to visit the United States to investigate this strange investment culture. They were intent on discovering whether all residents of Earth had lost the ability to recognize investment fiction from fact.

Upon arriving in the United States, they visited Wall Street and the New York Stock Exchange. After watching CNBC, the beings were convinced that their worst fears had been confirmed. There was, however, one hopeful being. She pleaded with the rest of the reconnaissance group that before they abandoned all hope they should find out what the legal statutes had to say about investment strategy. This would be a good test of what Earthlings truly believed about investing—at least those that took the time to study the evidence instead of listening to the hype. She convinced the group to visit the New York Public Library before heading back to their galaxy.

The beings visited the library after closing and scoured the legal reference section. They found that embedded within the American legal code is a doctrine known as the Prudent Investor Rule. They also found something called the Third Restatement of Trusts. The Restatement (Third), written in 1992 by the American Law Institute (ALI), made clear that it recognized that active management delivers inconsistent and poor results. They were especially happy to find that the ALI had the following to say about market efficiency:

- Economic evidence shows that the major capital markets of this country are highly efficient, in the sense that available information is rapidly digested and reflected in market prices.

- Fiduciaries and other investors are confronted with potent evidence that the application of expertise, investigation and diligence in efforts to "beat the market" ordinarily promises little or no payoff, or even a negative payoff after taking account of research and transaction costs.

- Empirical research supporting the theory of efficient markets reveals that in such markets skilled professionals have rarely been able to identify under-priced securities with any regularity.

- Evidence shows that there is little correlation between fund managers' earlier successes and their ability to produce above-market returns in subsequent periods.

They also found that there was something called the Uniform Prudent Investor Act. The Act governs the investment activities of trustees and is the law in virtually all states. They learned that the Act effectively makes passive investing the standard by which fiduciaries should be judged. They were pleased to see that the Act incorporated two important tenets of prudent investment management. The first is that because broad diversification is fundamental to the concept of risk management, it is incorporated into the definition of prudent investing. The second is that cost control is an essential part of prudent investing.

They also noted that the Act gives trustees the authority to delegate their responsibilities as a prudent investor would. Thus, trustees/investors who do not have the knowledge, skill, time or interest to prudently manage a portfolio should delegate that responsibility to an advisor who does.

They were also interested to find the following analysis from Michael G. Sher of the University of Minnesota's Carlson School of Management:

> "'Ethical malfeasance' occurs when an investment manager does something *deliberately* or *conceals it* (e.g., the manager knows that it's too drunk to drive, but drives anyway). For example, consider the manager who invests intentionally at a

118

higher level of risk than the client chose without informing the client and then subsequently generates a higher return than expected. ... The manager attributes the excess return to its superior investment skill [instead of the acceptance of incremental risk]."

"'Ethical misfeasance' occurs when an investment manager does something *by accident* (e.g., the manager really believes that it's sober enough to drive). ... Thus, the manager doesn't know what it's doing and shouldn't be managing money."

Sher concluded: "Managing money in an efficient market without investing passively is investment malfeasance." He then noted: "not knowing that such a market is efficient is investment misfeasance." In either case, he believed that "such conduct may be imprudent per se (i.e., there's no excuse for the manager to be driving)."[1] The bottom line is that Sher felt that passive investing is the more ethical way to invest.

After reading these various documents the beings realized that most investors did have ready access to the prudent investment approach. They felt assured that not all was lost. The beings left New York with the knowledge that investors need not accept the popular but flawed investment strategy of active management. They were pleased that investors were at least able to access the prudent investment alternative of passive asset class investing. However, they were sorry to see how long it was taking for the majority of Earth's investors to learn what they had known for thousands of years. They were also sad to see that so many of the yachts that were anchored in the marinas of lower Manhattan belonged to the brokers. They should have belonged to the investors.

The Moral of the Tale
The prudent investment strategy is available to all investors. All anyone needs to do is take a trip to the public library.

The next story discusses just how difficult it is to beat the market—even if you can forecast political and economic events with great accuracy.

It must be apparent to intelligent investors that if anyone possessed the ability to do so [forecast the immediate trend of stock prices] consistently and accurately he would become a billionaire so quickly he would not find it necessary to sell his stock market guesses to the general public.

—Weekly Staff Letter, August 27, 1951, David L. Babson & Company, quoted in Charles Ellis, *The Investor's Anthology*

Chapter 18:
Even With a Clear Crystal Ball

It was Thanksgiving Day 2003, but Tina was not in a festive mood. The papers finalizing her divorce had come in the mail the day before. Her thirty-year marriage to Tim was over. While Tina was not worried about her financial situation (the court having awarded her a $5 million settlement), she was feeling particularly vulnerable. She realized that she knew almost nothing about managing financial assets. Tim was the one who was interested in the market. She had left all of the investment decisions to him, but now that responsibility was hers. She had heard lots of tales of people being exploited by unscrupulous stockbrokers. She had to find someone she could trust.

Tina decided to call Bob Foreman, the attorney who had handled her divorce. She was hoping that Bob could recommend an advisor she could trust.

Bob: Tina, I know you must be concerned about finding someone you can trust. I can tell you that several of my clients, all women in similar situations, have been working with a local CPA that is also a registered investment advisor. I have known Sherman for twenty years and can certainly vouch for his character. He does my taxes and manages my investments. I would be glad to call him for you and have him set up an appointment.

Tina: That would be great. I really like the idea of having an accountant also serve as my financial advisor. A one-stop approach appeals to me. I would also appreciate it if you could give me the names of a few of the women that are using Sherman as their accountant and advisor. I prefer getting references from an independent source, rather than from the advisor. No one is going to give you references who are going to say negative things.

Bob: I would be happy to do that for you. But first I must call them and see if they are willing to speak to you.

Tina: That sounds great. I really appreciate your help.

The next day Sherman called Tina to introduce himself and set up an appointment. He told Tina that he was sending her the book, *What Wall Street Doesn't Want You to Know*. Reading the book was her homework assignment as preparation for the meeting. Sherman explained that the book would provide her with a basic understanding of the firm's investment philosophy. In addition, the book provided advice on how to choose an investment advisor.

That section would help her by providing a list of questions that she should ask of any advisor that she planned to interview. Tina thanked Sherman and agreed to read the book before their meeting.

Bob called later that day with the names of three women who had hired Sherman as their accountant and financial advisor. Tina heard from each of them that they were extremely pleased with Sherman as their advisor. They told her that Sherman worked hard to educate them about investing. He made sure that they not only participated in the decision-making process, but after carefully explaining the pros and cons of various alternatives he left the final decision to them. He would then play devil's advocate to make sure that they fully understood the risks before implementing anything. Tina liked what she heard and was looking forward to the meeting.

Over the course of the next two weeks, Tina read the book and took copious notes. She knew that the choice of an investment advisor was going to be one of the most important decisions she would make. She wanted to do everything she could to ensure that she made the right decision. She knew that the wrong decision could not only prove costly, but it would be one from which she might not be able to recover. With help from the book, she came to the meeting prepared with a long list of due diligence questions.

As far as Tina was concerned, the meeting could not have gone any better. Sherman not only did a great job explaining the firm's philosophy and how he worked with clients, but he also listened carefully to her concerns and satisfactorily answered her questions. She told Sherman that she would like to work with him.

Over the course of the next few weeks Tina and Sherman held several meetings. Right after the new year a meeting was scheduled to finalize and implement the plan. At the meeting Sherman explained to her that based on her assets of $5 million, she could prudently plan on being able to withdraw living expenses of $150,000 per annum, which was 3 percent of the current value of her assets. The amount would then be adjusted each year to take inflation into account. That was good news as it was more than sufficient to allow her to maintain her current lifestyle.

By the end of the meeting, Tina was confident that together they had developed an overall financial plan that addressed all of her financial needs, including such issues as long-term health care and other types of insurance. Her investment plan was also integrated into an estate and tax plan. There was only one issue that was making her rather nervous.

Tina: Sherman, I have been comfortable with the entire process and I have confidence in you. Having said that, I am extremely nervous about investing

$5 million dollars at one time when all I am hearing on the radio and television and reading in the papers is that now is a risky time to be in the market. The news is filled with the problems of a jobless recovery, outsourcing of jobs, huge budget and trade deficits and how the sharp rise in the price of oil is hurting the economy. And then there are the problems in the Middle East and the escalating problems of terrorism as it spreads around the globe. And aren't interest rates set to rise sharply? Is now really a good time to invest?

Sherman: I am glad you asked that question. First, it is important to acknowledge that there are always risks when investing. Second, as I told you at our first meeting, everything we do is based on academic evidence, not on my opinions. So let me tell you about the evidence on the ability of people to forecast the economy.

William Sherden is the author of a wonderful book *The Fortune Sellers*. If you are interested in reading it, I am happy to lend you our copy. Sherden was inspired by the following incident to write his book. In 1985, when preparing testimony as an expert witness, he analyzed the track records of inflation projections by different forecasting methods. He then compared those forecasts to what is called the "naive" forecast—simply projecting today's inflation rate into the future. He was surprised to learn that the simple naive forecast proved to be the most accurate, beating the forecasts of the most prestigious economic forecasting firms equipped with their Ph.D.s from leading universities and thousand-equation computer models.

Sherden then reviewed the leading research on forecasting accuracy from 1979 to 1995 and covering forecasts made from 1970 to 1995. He concluded that:

- *Economists cannot predict the turning points in the economy.* Of the forty-eight predictions made by economists, forty-six missed the turning points.

- *Economists' forecasting skill is about as good as guessing.* For example, even the economists who directly or indirectly run the economy— the Federal Reserve, the Council of Economic Advisors and the Congressional Budget—had forecasting records that were worse than pure chance.

- *There are no economic forecasters who consistently lead the pack in forecasting accuracy.*

- *There are no economic ideologies whose adherents produce consistently superior economic forecasts.*

• *Increased sophistication provides no improvement in economic fore-casting accuracy.*

• *Consensus forecasts offer little improvement.*

• *Forecasts may be affected by psychological bias.* Some economists are perpetually optimistic and others perpetually pessimistic.[1]

Since the underlying basis of most stock market forecasts is an economic forecast, the evidence suggests that stock market strategists who predict bull and bear markets will have no greater success than do the economists.

Now let me give you a concrete example of why you should treat all prognostications about the stock market as nothing more than what I call investment graffiti. It will demonstrate that even if you have a clear crystal ball, and are thus able to foresee events (though not stock prices) that will occur in the future with perfect clarity, you should still avoid trying to time the market. As you consider this example, keep in mind that Sherden's study demonstrated that no one in the real world has that perfectly clear crystal ball.

Let's review what happened to the equity markets in 2003. To begin, it was the best year for equity investors in the last quarter century. Not since 1975–76, when global markets were recovering from the bear market of 1973–74, did investors earn such high returns. U.S. large-cap stocks rose in excess of 25 percent. U.S. large value and real estate investment trusts rose in excess of 30 percent. International large value stocks rose in excess of 40 percent. U.S. small-cap, international small-cap, and emerging market stocks all rose in excess of 50 percent. U.S. microcap stocks and international small value stocks rose in excess of 60 percent. And emerging market value stocks rose in excess of 70 percent. Most of our clients have some exposure to all of these asset classes.

It is important to point out, however, that almost no one, if anyone, fore-casted a bull market in 2003, let alone the kind of returns that were actually experienced. And if any investor had a clear crystal ball, allowing him or her to foresee the events that would occur in 2003, they almost surely would have forecasted a bear, not a bull market. I know I would have.

Let's review some of the major events that occurred. Not only would we go to war in Iraq without U.N. support, but the markets would also have to deal with the ongoing uncertainty that has existed since we declared military victory. The markets would also have to deal with an outbreak of SARS, corporate scandals, mutual fund scandals, record trade and budget deficits, a renegade North Korea, an escalation of the Palestinian-Israeli conflict, the threat of deflation and a "jobless" recovery.

As you can see, even if you had a clear crystal ball as to the news events that would impact the market it would have done you little good. In fact, in all likelihood, it would have hurt you. You would almost surely have missed one of the great bull markets of all time. Thus, the conclusion I draw, and I hope you will agree, is that you should ignore—or at least treat only as entertainment (because their crystal balls certainly are not clear)—the market forecasts of Wall Street strategists. Perhaps my example will help you appreciate the old joke that there are only three types of market forecasters: those that don't know where the market is going; those that don't know that they don't know where the market is going; and those that know they don't know, but get paid a lot of money to pretend that they do know.

We have developed a well-thought-out plan and we should not allow, now or ever, the noise of the market to distract us from that plan.

Tina: Thanks for the explanation, but I am still nervous about investing the entire $5 million all at once. Do I have to do that?

Sherman: No you don't. I will explain the alternatives and, as always, provide you with the academic evidence on which is the most likely to prove to be the best choice. Let's begin with the fixed income portion of your assets. If you recall our conversation, based on the academic evidence and your need for cash flow, we are going to invest that portion of your portfolio in very high quality and relatively short-term instruments. These types of investments entail little risk. Thus, I see no reason to leave money on the table, which is what we would be doing if we kept those assets in a money market account until you feel better about the investment environment. Since you have little need to take risk, the fixed income assets account for 60 percent of the portfolio, or $3 million. So I suggest we invest that immediately.

Tina: That sounds fine.

Sherman: Great. I will place the order to invest those funds right after we conclude the meeting. Now let's address the $2 million of equities we plan to invest. From an academic perspective the answer is simple. Since the market rises a majority of the time, you should invest it all now. If you do otherwise, the likely result is that you will eventually buy at higher prices. Unfortunately, people don't always base investment decisions on logic. In fact, when it comes to investing my experience is that the stomach often plays a greater role in decision-making than the mind. One of the most important roles I play is to

125

make sure that, as much as possible, you are allowing your mind to make decisions, not your stomach.

It is my experience that almost all investors, faced with the same situation with which you are confronted, are sure that if they were to take the plunge and invest all at one time, that day would turn out to be a peak which the market would not exceed until the next millennium. This causes them to delay the decision altogether, with often paralyzing results. If the market rises after they delay, they feel that if they couldn't buy at what they felt was too high a price, how can they buy now at even higher prices. If the market falls, they feel that they can't buy now because the bear market they feared has now arrived. The problem they face is this: Once a decision has been made to not buy, exactly how do you make the decision to buy?

I believe that there is a good solution to this dilemma, one that addresses both the logic and the emotional issues. I recommend that if you cannot get yourself to invest all at once, we write down a plan to which you will agree to adhere. The plan will lay out a schedule with regularly planned investments. The following are three alternatives I suggest you consider.

- Invest one-third of the investment immediately and invest the remainder one-third at a time over the next two months or next two quarters.

- Invest one-quarter today and invest the remainder spread equally over the next three months or quarters.

- Invest one-sixth each month for six months or every other month.

I have suggested a maximum of one year because the longer the schedule, the more likely it is that you will miss out on market gains. What do you think?

Tina: I understand the logic of the take-the-plunge approach, but I just feel more comfortable going a bit slower. I will sleep better that way. I like the idea of investing one-quarter now and then the remainder spread equally over the next three quarters.

Sherman: I am going to have this written up and ask you to sign a document authorizing me to make those investments as you have instructed me to do. I want you to know that I am going to implement the plan regardless of how the market performs. Are you okay with that?

Tina: Yes, I understand.

Sherman: Great. I have another suggestion regarding this plan. I suggest that you now adopt a "glass is half-full" perspective. If the market rises after we make the initial investment, you are going to feel good about how your port-folio has performed. You are going to congratulate yourself for being smart to not have delayed investing. If, on the other hand, the market has fallen, you are going to feel good about the opportunity you now have to buy more at lower prices. You will also congratulate yourself for being smart, or lucky, enough not to have put all of your money in at one time. Either way you are going to win, at least from a psychological perspective. Can you do that?

Tina: I think so. And, more importantly, I understand the message.

Sherman: I have just one more question for you. Tomorrow we are going to invest one-fourth of your $2 million. After tomorrow, are you going to root for the stock market to go up or down?

Tina: Why up, of course!

Sherman: No Tina, you should actually root for it to go down. The reason is that we are going to be buying more in the future and I am sure you will agree that it is better to be able to buy at lower, rather than higher, prices. If the market falls, that is exactly what we will be able to do.

Tina: I see, but I am not sure I can root for the market to go down.

Sherman: I really don't expect you to, but you can see that it will actually help us in the long-term if that is what occurs. With this knowledge, perhaps you will feel better about a bear market if that is what happens. Do you have any more questions?

Tina: No, I'm ready.

Sherman: I want you to feel free to call with any type of question. I am not on any clock in terms of the fees you pay. I'll be calling you shortly after the end of the quarter to set up a meeting. You'll receive an agenda ahead of time for you to review. If you want to add anything, just let me know. You will also receive a quarterly portfolio analysis report for review prior to the meeting. I may even make some comments on it for you to consider.

At each meeting I am going to ask you if anything has changed in your life that would cause us to want to revisit the assumptions we used in developing the plan. I will also ask you how you are feeling about the markets and how your portfolio is doing. That will help me address any issues about which you might be concerned. We will also review the performance of the portfolio to see if we are on track to meet your long-term goals, or if any adjustments need to be made. We will also check to see if the market has moved in such a way to cause our asset allocations to drift away from the desired percentages. If that is the case, we will decide if any rebalancing is needed and how best to accomplish it. And, we will also check for any opportunities to take a loss for tax purposes as "harvesting losses" reduces your overall tax bill. And then we will discuss whatever other issues you feel are important. How does that sound?

Tina: This has been great. I really feel comfortable now.

Sherman: Thanks. I appreciate your trust and confidence.

The Moral of the Tale

Casey Stengel, generally considered one of the greatest of baseball managers, was known to have said: "Forecasting is very difficult, especially if it involves the future." Even if you had a crystal ball that allowed you to foretell future events, timing the market would still likely be a loser's game. The winning strategy is to adhere to a well-thought-out plan and ignore the noise of the market.

The next tale is another about the value of economic forecasts. As you read the tale keep in mind that most market forecasts are based on economic forecasts.

Chapter 19:
Be Careful What You Ask For

According to Greek mythology, Midas was a wealthy king of Phrygia. One day the Satyr Silenus —a beast that was half man, half goat, and the tutor of Dionysos, the god of wine—lost his way and stumbled upon Midas and his palace. The King extended to Silenus his hospitality. Upon discovering this kindness, Dionysos granted Midas a wish. Midas asked that everything he touched would turn to gold. Midas reveled in his gift, thinking he would become the richest man in the world. His foolishness quickly became apparent. In hunger and despair he embraced his young daughter for comfort, only to find that she too turned to gold. Midas begged Dionysos to take his golden touch away. Eventually the god relented and his daughter was restored to life.[1]

For today's investors, the equivalent of the "Midas touch" might be the ability to forecast economic growth rates. If you could forecast with 100 percent certainty which countries would have the highest growth rates you could invest in them, avoiding the countries with low growth rates. And that would lead to abnormal profits. Or, perhaps not.

This is the question Jim Davis of Dimensional Fund Advisors sought to answer in a 2006 study on emerging markets that covered the period 1990–2005.[2] He chose the emerging markets because the widely held perception is that the markets of the emerging countries are inefficient.

Davis evenly divided the emerging market countries in the IFC Investable Universe database into two groups based on GDP growth for the upcoming year. The high-growth group consisted of the 50 percent of the countries with the highest real GDP growth for the year. He then measured returns using two sets of country weights—aggregate free-float-adjusted market-cap weights and equal weights. (Free-float refers to the amount of a company's shares outstanding available for purchase on the open market at any point in time.) Companies were market-cap weighted within countries. The results are shown in the following table for the period from 1990 to 2005.

	Market-Cap Weighted Countries	Equally Weighted Countries
	Average Annual Return	Average Annual Return
High-Growth Countries	16.4%	22.6%
Low-Growth Countries	16.4%	21.5%

It seems that there is not much, if any, advantage to know in advance which countries will have the highest rates of GDP growth. The conclusion that we can draw is that the emerging markets are very much like the rest of the world's capital markets—they do an excellent job of reflecting economic growth prospects into stock prices. The only advantage would come from being able to forecast *surprises* in growth rates. For example, if a country was forecasted by the market to have 6 percent GDP growth, and you accurately forecasted a rate of growth of 7 percent, you might have been able to exploit such information (depending on how much it cost to make the forecasts and how much it cost to execute the strategy). As you have already seen, there does not seem to be any evidence of the ability to forecast GDP rates any better than do the markets.

Investors make the same mistake when they buy stocks that have high expected earnings growth because they believe that the high growth in earnings will result in high returns. The evidence is that there is no such connection. As we have discussed, companies with high rates of earnings growth (growth stocks) actually produce lower returns than ones with low earnings growth rates (value stocks). The reason is that markets price risk as well as expected growth rates. High *expected* growth rates are already built into current prices, just as high expected GDP growth rates of countries are built into *current* stock prices.

The Moral of the Tale
It seems intuitive that if you could accurately forecast which countries would have high GDP growth rates that you would be able to exploit that knowledge and earn abnormal returns. The same intuition applies to the ability to forecast which companies will have high growth of earnings. In both cases, relying on intuition leads to an incorrect conclusion. The reason is that markets are highly efficient in building information about future prospects into prices. And it is only surprises, which by definition are unpredictable, that provide an advantage. Obviously forecasting is not free. There are costs (research expenses) involved in making the forecasts. And there are costs involved in trying to

exploit those forecasts (operating expenses, trading costs and taxes related to turnover). The evidence is that the efforts and expenditures only serve to reduce returns, not enhance them. Thus, the moral of our story is that the premise upon which much of active management is based is a false one.

The next tale is also about the value of economic forecasts. If you are not already convinced that the winning strategy is to ignore all such forecasts, this one should "put a nail in that coffin."

If I have noticed anything over these sixty years on Wall Street, it is that people do not succeed in forecasting what's going to happen to the stock market.

—Benjamin Graham, legendary investor and author, *Security Analysis*

Chapter 20:
Ship of Fools

Today we know that astronomy and astrology are entirely different fields. Astronomy is a *science*. Astronomers are scientists who study matter in outer space, especially the positions, dimensions, distribution, motion, composition, energy and evolution of celestial bodies and phenomena.

Astrology is not a science. Astrologers study the positions and aspects of celestial bodies believing that the stars have an influence on the course of natural earthly occurrences and human affairs. Prior to about 1750, even some of the great astronomers (e.g., Tycho Brahe and Johannes Kepler) were also astrologers. It was not until about 1750 that the two fields finally diverged.

Despite the overwhelming body of evidence that economic and market forecasts have as much value as astrologic forecasts, too many investors still treat such forecasts as if they came from the equivalent of astronomers, instead of astrologers. Hopefully, after considering this tale, you will no longer make that mistake.

All Clear on the Starboard Bow?

"The Federal Reserve finally passed its much anticipated rate hike. Consider this 0.25 percent move as a warning shot over the bow for investors." This was the opening line from the July 1, 2004 cbsmarketwatch.com column of William E. Donoghue, dubbed by one financial writer as "the father of safe money investing." Donoghue's Web site states that he is a "forty-year veteran independent investment expert, the leading advocate of successful proactive investment management and sector rotation strategies which have produced world-class returns for investors in both bull and bear markets."

Captain, My Captain

In his column, Donoghue went on to warn investors not to "go down with the ship." With the old catch-phrase being that one should not "fight the Fed," Donoghue advised investors to anticipate rising interest rates and "pull out of fixed-income mutual funds, which are *guaranteed* to take on water as interest rates rise higher. Long-term government bond funds and zero-coupon bond funds are the most vulnerable in the intermediate term. It's just *foolish* not to take advantage of inverse bond funds, given the current environment (emphasis mine)." He continued: "Rates rise and the 'safest' investments (most credit-worthy) will lose the most market value. Among the worst investments to hold as interest rates rise will be long-term U.S. Treasury bonds, zero-coupon bonds, utility stocks, blue-chip stocks, and index funds. The best buy-and-hold investment might be an inverse bond fund or bear market stock fund." And he advised to dump the others as they were virtually guaranteed losers. And if that was insufficient to scare you into action he concluded: "Smart money investors are selling long-term government bond exchange-traded funds short by a huge margin. So why are your advisors still counseling, 'stay the course'?"

Donoghue advised investors to seek profits from rising interest rates, falling bond values and falling stock values by purchasing the shares of three "bear market" mutual funds:

- Rydex Inverse Government Bond Fund (RYJUX). The objective of the fund is to increase in value by 100 percent of what the most recent long Treasury bond loses.

- Profunds Rising Rates Opportunity Fund (RRPIX). The objective of the fund is to earn 125 percent of the same move.

- Direxion 10-Year Note Bear (DXKSX)—formerly Potomac ContraBond Fund. The objective of the fund is to earn 200 percent of what the 10-year Treasury bond loses.

Before we go to "the videotape" to see the results of this guru's recommendations, let's review the Federal Reserve's actions. In this regard, Donoghue's forecast was accurate. The Fed went on to raise rates sixteen more times by the end of June 2006. Surely his recommendations benefited from his perfectly clear crystal ball. Or did they? The following are the results for the twelve months following his recommendations: DXKSX -13.3 percent; RYJUX -17.5 percent; and RRPIX -22.0 percent. On the other hand Vanguard's Total Bond Market Index Fund returned +6.8 percent and its Total Stock Market Index Fund returned +8.0 percent.

The following year, assuming investors had the courage of Donoghue's convictions (how many would have stayed the course in the face of such disastrous results?), turned out better. The following are the returns for the twelve months ending June 30, 2006: DXKSX +20.6 percent; RYJUX +19.3 percent; and RRPIX +23.8 percent. The Vanguard bond fund lost 1 percent while its total stock market fund returned +9.8 percent. Unfortunately, Donoghue made his forecast in July 2004, not July 2005.

The cumulative results for the full two-year period certainly don't reflect the boast of "world class returns in bull and bear markets." The three funds recommended by Donoghue returned +4.6 percent (DXKSX), -1.6 percent (RYJUX), and –3.4 percent (RRPIX), respectively. During the same period the Vanguard Total Bond Market Index Fund and its Total Stock Market Index Fund (both virtually guaranteed to be losers by Donoghue) returned +5.6 percent and +18.5 percent, respectively.

Walking the Plank

After seventeen consecutive interest rate hikes, Vanguard's Total Bond Fund and its Total Stock Fund were both beating all three inverse bond funds. And, if an investor had purchased an inverse stock fund based on Donoghue's recommendation, he would have experienced significant losses. Even with the benefit of having his economic forecast turn out as expected, Donoghue's recommendations still proved ill-advised for investors who followed his advice. This is why investors should treat economic and market forecasts by so-called "experts" (gurus) as investment graffiti—the only value they have is as perhaps entertainment.

The Moral of the Tale

The moral of this tale is that the next time some guru's forecast tempts you to stray from your well-thought-out investment plan, no matter how well reasoned the arguments may seem, the prudent action is to ignore them. And if you are tempted, reread this tale to remind yourself why staying the course is the winner's game.

The next story is about identifying the winning investment strategy.

There are trends that have been major market drivers for the decade. Indexing people are looking to reduce costs, control exposures to the marketplace and to get exact implementation of pension policies. They are fed up with out-of-control outcomes.

—Frederick Grauer, former co-chairman of Barclays Global Investors

Chapter 21:
What If Everyone Indexed?

Howard was careful and deliberate in everything he did. And that certainly pertained to investing. Over lunch with his friend Roy, Howard mentioned that he was unhappy with the performance of his portfolio. Over the years he had hired and fired a number of investment advisors and money managers. All of them had shown him great returns *before* he had hired them. Unfortunately, the returns he earned *after* hiring these firms rarely matched the kind of returns their track records suggested they would deliver. Roy told Howard that, coincidentally, he had just come from a quarterly meeting with his advisor. He thought Howard would enjoy meeting with him.

Roy explained that the approach his advisor used was totally different from the one Howard had been employing. It went against the conventional wisdom that the way to investment riches is to pick great stocks and time the market and/or hire great managers that would do that for you. The strategy was instead based on Modern Portfolio Theory, the Efficient Markets Hypothesis and passive asset class investing. Roy mentioned how he was pleased with the approach and the results.

Roy then pulled out of his briefcase the quarterly report he had just reviewed with his advisor. Roy showed Howard that his portfolio, while producing good returns during the late 1990s, did not do as well as if he had limited his investments to the type of stocks most investors held as the majority of their portfolio—U.S. large-cap growth stocks. His portfolio was much more diversified. He did not have all his eggs in one basket.

While the glamour U.S. large growth stocks were rising an average of about 31 percent a year from 1995 through 1999, his more diversified portfolio was averaging returns of about 17 percent a year. However, while many of his friends had suffered severe losses in the bear market of 2000–02, he had about broken even. Even his equities had produced small but positive returns in the first two years of that bear market. And they only lost about 10 percent in the severe bear market of 2002. In 2003, however, the equity portion of his portfolio was up almost 50 percent. If he considered the whole time frame, his portfolio had not only outperformed the market, but he had enjoyed a smoother ride. He had not suffered from anywhere near the level of stomach acid that many of his friends had experienced. Howard was quite impressed.

Roy gave Howard a copy of *The Successful Investor Today: 14 Simple Truths You Must Know When You Invest* and said: "Here, why don't you read this. I am sure it will do a better job of explaining the investment approach than I could. Just give it back to me when you are finished reading it. If you are interested in learning more, my advisor's name and number are on the inside cover. If you call, just tell him I recommended that you call."

Howard read the book and found both the logic and evidence compelling. For the first time he began to understand why his investment strategies, and those of the managers he hired, never seemed to deliver on their great promise. He was interested to learn more about the strategy and specifically how the advisor worked with clients. He also had one question that he really wanted the advisor to answer: What would happen if everyone adopted a passive approach? What if everyone indexed?

Howard called the advisor, Jim Smith, after reading the book. At the meeting, Jim explained both the theory upon which the firm based its investment philosophy and also how the firm worked with clients. Howard told him that it all sounded great and he really only had one question. Could he explain what would happen if everyone indexed? Specifically, would a passive strategy still work? The conversation proceeded as follow.

Jim: Well, let's begin with the fact that we are a long way from that happening—even at the current pace of change. First, institutions probably now have in the neighborhood of just 40 percent of their assets committed to passive strategies. By comparison, while more and more individual investors are shifting to passive investing, it is estimated that individuals still have about 90 percent of their assets in individual stocks and actively managed funds. Second, even if every investor adopted a passive strategy, there would always be some trading activity from the exercise of stock options, estates being liquidated, divorces, mergers and acquisitions, etc. Also remember that even if individuals stopped trading stocks, companies would still be active in buying other companies. With that in mind let's deal with the real issue—the likelihood of active managers either gaining or losing an advantage as the trend toward passive management marches on.

Let's first address the issue of information efficiency. With less active management activity, there will be fewer professionals researching and recommending securities. Active management proponents would argue that it would, therefore, be easier to gain a competitive advantage. This is the same argument they currently make about the markets for small-cap stocks and emerging market stocks: they are inefficient. Unfortunately for active managers their underperformance against proper benchmarks has been just as great, if not more so, in these asset classes as it has been in the large-cap arena. One of the reasons, and perhaps the main reason, is that in these "inefficient" asset classes the costs of trading, both in terms of bid-offer spreads and market impact costs, are much greater than they are in the large-cap asset class.

Less efficient markets are typically characterized by lower trading volumes. The lower trading activity results in less liquidity and therefore greater trading costs. As more investors move to passive strategies it is logical to conclude that trading activity would decline. Interestingly, while we have seen a shift to passive management by both individuals and institutions, trading volumes continue to set new records. We can conclude that the remaining active participants are becoming more active—increasing their turnover (and their costs). However, if, as investors shifted to passive management trading, activity fell, liquidity would decline and trading costs would rise. The increase in trading costs would raise the already substantial hurdle that active managers have to overcome to outperform.

Based on the evidence we have on both "inefficient" small-cap stocks and emerging market stocks, it seems likely that any information advantage gained by a lessening of competition for information would be offset by an increase in trading costs. If you recall, that evidence was presented in the book Roy gave to you. Remember for active management to be the winning strategy it is a necessary, but not sufficient, condition that the markets are inefficient. The other condition is that the costs of implementing an active strategy must be small enough that market inefficiencies can be exploited, after expenses.

There is another interesting conclusion that can be drawn about the trend toward passive investing. Remember that for active managers to win, they must exploit the mistakes of others. Before we go into that issue I would like to present you with a problem from game theory. I think you will find it interesting. I will then come back and relate the problem to investment strategy.

Imagine the following scenario: You are an NBA player. The league is holding a free-throw shooting contest open to all players. Each participating player will shoot one hundred free throws. Players will receive $100 for each free throw they make. They are also given the choice of either participating in the contest or accepting the average score of all players who do participate. The best free-throw shooter in the league shoots about 90 percent, the average player shoots just 65 percent, and you shoot a better than average 80 percent. Howard, the question for you is: Should you compete, or should you choose not to play and accept the average score of all players who do participate?

Howard: Well, I can expect to hit 80 percent of my shots. And while it is not certain I would win $8,000, that is what I should expect to win. On the other hand, if I take the average score, I should expect to win just $6,500. I guess I should play the game.

Jim: That sounds quite logical. But let's see if that is the correct answer. While the obvious answer would seem to be that you should play, game theory provides a different answer. Howard, the fact that you are an above-average shooter is not really relevant to the problem. Here is why. Knowing that he is probably the worst free-throw shooter in the league, Shaquille O'Neal would clearly be better off not participating. Not being a fool, he decides to accept the average score. All the other weak shooters quickly come to the same conclusion. Thus, the average score of the remaining players starts to rise. Anticipating this occurrence, the weakest of the remaining players logically drops out as well. This process would repeat itself until you are the weakest player left. At that point you too should decide not to play. The reason is that the remaining players would all have a higher historical shooting percentage than you. This process would continue until only one player would remain, the best shooter in the league. This is the thought process that is logical. Only the best should compete. All others should accept the average score, which now has an expected return of $9,000.

What does this problem and game theory have to do with deciding on whether active or passive investing is the winning strategy? I think we can agree that it seems likely that those abandoning active management in favor of passive strategies will be investors who have had poor experiences with active investing. The reason this seems logical is that it doesn't seem likely that an individual would abandon a winning strategy. The only other logical explanation I can come up with is that an individual simply recognized that they had been lucky. That conclusion would be inconsistent with behavioral studies that show that individuals tend to take credit for their success as skill based while they attribute failures to bad luck. Thus, it seems logical to conclude that the remaining players are likely to be the ones with the most skill. Therefore, we can conclude that as the "less skilled" investors abandon active strategies, the remaining competition is likely to get tougher and tougher—just as in the example of the free-throw shooting contest. Thus, unless you happen to be Warren Buffett (the equivalent of the best free-throw shooter), the winning strategy is not to play. Instead the winning strategy is to accept market returns.

Howard, while it is unlikely that everyone will abandon active strategies—after all hope does spring eternal—I see nothing in the trend to passive investing that gives reason for optimism among the believers in active management. In fact, just the opposite appears to be true.

Howard: Thanks for answering my question. What are the next steps we need to take to move forward?

The Moral the Tale
Understanding the skill level of the competition is important in determining the winning strategy.

The next story demonstrates why it is important to be able to differentiate entertainment from prudent investment advice.

If you're having fun investing, then there's a good chance that you're not properly diversified, you're trading too much, and you're taking too much risk.

—Gregory Baer and Gary Gensler, *The Great Mutual Fund Trap*

Chapter 22:
Mad Money

Millions of people each year visit Las Vegas. With the exception of a small percent of professional gamblers, the casinos are filled with tourists eager to test their luck. Knowing that the odds favor the house, while they hope to win, they expect to lose. The expected loss from gambling is, in effect, the price of entertainment. Of course, that entertainment not only includes what happens at the gaming tables and the roulette wheels, but also the great singers, comedians, magicians, and spectacular shows from Cirque du Soleil. There are also many fantastic restaurants.

While perfectly willing to spend their hard earned dollars on entertainment, most visitors know that it would not be prudent to invest their savings at the gambling tables—they are able to separate entertainment from investing. Once they return home, however, this is not always the case.

Jim Cramer, ex-hedge fund manager and co-founder of TheStreet.com, has become one of the most recognizable faces in the investment world. He dispenses rapid-fire investment advice on the show "Mad Money." Since it premiered in March 2005, it has been one of CNBC's most watched shows. In September 2005, *Variety* reported that, "The freewheeling investor show hosted by Jim Cramer, increased the net's 6 p.m. [performance] by 141% in the third quarter and became the financial net's highest-rated show in primetime."[1]

But has it been as successful for the investors who follow his advice? Three PhD students at Northwestern University's Kellogg School of Management sought the answer to this question in their 2006 paper, "Is the Market Mad? Evidence from Mad Money."[2]

At first glance, the answer would appear to be yes. Typically, after Cramer recommended a stock, its volume soared. For example, the authors found that on the smallest quartile of stocks, volume was almost nine times more than on the day after his recommendation (and stayed above normal for about three days, with the effect decreasing with time). The increased demand led to an overnight rise in prices of about 5 percent for the smallest stocks (where they can have the greatest impact) and about 2 percent for the entire sample of the 246 unconditional recommendations examined between July 28, 2005 and October 14, 2005.

Unfortunately, those gains turned out to be temporary. For example, price gains for stocks in the smallest quartile completely reversed within twelve trading days. The original gains turned into nothing more than market impact costs. In other words, after costs, Cramer's picks typically had negative value to naïve investors who reacted to the buy recommendations.

However, because the market is so efficient, a different category of investors may have benefited from Cramer's picks. For example, while the demand for Cramer's stock picks increased, there was also an increase in the volume of short selling (bets that the stocks will fall). In the opening minutes of the day following one of his recommendations, short sales increased to almost seven times their normal levels, and they remained elevated for three days.

Besides individuals who followed Cramer's show, the authors identified two main players: "the market makers who supply liquidity to these investors, and the arbitrageurs who attempt to profit from the mispricing following the recommendations."[3]

The authors also found that the stocks that Cramer recommended had excess returns for the three days prior to his actual recommendation. They provided two explanations for this behavior. Their first explanation was that Cramer was recommending stocks with short-term momentum (of which there is some evidence, although after trading costs the positive momentum would be difficult, if not impossible, to exploit). Their second explanation was that information pertaining to some of the stocks he recommended was released before the television show aired each day (during market hours), which the authors attributed to either Cramer's daily radio show or Web columns.

Instead of following pied pipers such as Cramer, investors should adhere to a prudent investment plan based on their long-term financial goals and risk tolerance. Cramer might be providing entertainment for those who enjoy screaming, chair throwing, ringing cash registers and shouting "Booyah." While this might make for enjoyable television, it also falls into the category of active management (market timing and individual stock selection). Copious academic research has indicated active management is unlikely to offer persistent outperformance, particularly after accounting for the cost of implementation.

Cramer and CNBC attempt to make investing entertaining. After all, the goal of any television show is to attract the greatest number of viewers. But investing should not be considered a form of entertainment. Instead, investing should be about taking the appropriate amount of risk (with commensurate expected returns) to achieve well-defined long-term financial goals. It should be about forming a careful plan for achieving those goals, and remaining adherent to it in a highly disciplined manner. Research shows that, on average, investors harm themselves with too-frequent trading—often a result of paying attention to what they believe is valuable information but is really nothing more than Cramer-style "noise."

The Moral of the Tale

The moral of this tale is that while it is fine to render unto Caesar's Palace your entertainment dollar, you should not be rendering unto Wall Street your investment dollars. While Cramer might be providing entertainment, those following his recommendations are like lambs being led to be sheared by more sophisticated institutional investors.

Both CNBC and Cramer attempt to make investing entertaining so you will pay attention. And, they hope you forget that your actions make them money. However, investing was never meant to be entertaining. Instead, it should be about giving yourself the greatest chance to achieve your goals with the least amount of risk. Research shows that investors harm themselves, on average, with every trade inspired by paying attention to what is actually nothing more than "noise" (which Cramer certainly makes a lot of). The prudent strategy is thus to develop a well-thought-out plan and to have the discipline to adhere to it, ignoring the noise of the market, whether it comes from Jim Cramer or any other prognosticator. As Steve Forbes, publisher of the magazine that bears his name stated: "You make more money selling the advice than following it."[4]

The next story explains why passive investing is the winning strategy in life as well as investing.

As I traipse around the country speaking to investing groups, or just stay in my cage writing my articles, I'm often accused of "disempowering" people because I refuse to give any credence to anyone's hope of beating the market. The knowledge that I don't need to know anything is an incredibly profound form of knowledge. Personally, I think it's the ultimate form of empowerment. You can't tune out the massive industry of investment prediction unless you want to: otherwise, you'll never have the fortitude to stop listening. But if you can plug your ears to every attempt (by anyone) to predict what the markets will do, you will outperform nearly every other investor alive over the long run. Only the mantra of "don't know, and I don't care" will get you there.

—Jason Zweig

Chapter 23:
The Big Rocks

An expert in time management was speaking to a group of graduate business students. After a brief introduction she produced a large mason jar and set it on the table. Then she brought out a box filled with big rocks. She removed the rocks from the box and began to carefully place them, one at a time, into the jar. When no more rocks would fit inside the jar, she asked the class, "Is this jar full?" Everyone yelled, "Yes." She replied, "Oh really?"

She pulled out a bucket of gravel from under the table and dumped some into the jar. Pieces of gravel moved into the spaces between the big rocks. She continued this process until no more gravel could be placed into the jar. She asked again, "Is the jar full?" One student answered, "Probably not."

She then reached under the table, brought out a bucket of sand, and dumped the sand into the jar. The sand began to fill the spaces between the rocks and the gravel. She continued until no more sand could fit into the jar. Once again she asked, "Is this jar full?" Everyone shouted, "No!"

Finally, she filled the jar with water and asked, "What is the point of this demonstration?" An eager student said, "The point is that no matter how full your schedule is, you can always fit in one more meeting!"

Once the laughter had died down, the speaker replied, "That's not the point. This demonstration teaches us that if you don't put in the big rocks first, you'll never get them into the jar at all. What are the big rocks in your life? Time with your loved ones, your faith, your education, your dreams, your career, a worthy cause, teaching or mentoring others?" She concluded by repeating the important message: "Remember to put these big rocks in first, or you'll never get them in at all."

Individual investors following an active management strategy spend much of their precious leisure time watching the latest business news, studying the latest charts, scanning and posting on Internet investment discussion boards, reading financial trade publications and newsletters, and so on. What they are really doing is focusing on the gravel, the sand and the water, leaving insufficient time for the big rocks. On the other hand, investors who adopt a passive investment strategy ignore the "noise," (the sand, the gravel and the water). They are playing the winner's game and focusing on the big rocks, the really important things in their lives.

Consider these words of wisdom from Paul Samuelson, probably the most famous economist of our time: "You shouldn't spend much time on your investments. That will just tempt you to pull up your plants and see how the roots are doing, and that's bad for the roots. It's also very bad for your sleep."[1] The following true story demonstrates these points better than a fictional story would.

Shortly after my first book on Modern Portfolio Theory and passive investing as the winning strategy was published in 1998, a doctor called and related this story. He had been in practice a few years and had a wife, a young child and one more on the way. Many of his friends had generated large profits from trading stocks and he became caught up in the euphoria of the bull market.

After putting in a long day at the office he would come home to his computer and the Internet. He spent hours studying charts and investment reports and following the chat boards. He was caught up in the excitement of the bull market, a technology revolution that was changing the world, access to information that the Internet provided, the hype surrounding the success of day traders, and so on. The expansion of the coverage of financial markets by the financial media helped fuel the interest in active management and the "take control of your portfolio" mentality. Within just a few months he had turned his small initial investment into about $100,000.

Unfortunately, his wife no longer saw her husband and his child no longer had a father; the doctor was now "married" to his computer and his investments. His wife began to seriously question their marriage. *Luckily*, he lost all his profits within a few months.

Fortunately, the doctor recognized that he was not paying attention to the most important part of his life — his family. He also realized that his original gains were a result of luck, similar to a hot hand at the craps table. Someone suggested that he read my book, *The Only Guide to a Winning Investment Strategy You'll Ever Need*. After doing so, he called to thank me. He told me that he recognized his error and had designed a portfolio of index funds and sworn off active investing.

The following is another true story. It is another that made me realize how adopting passive investing as the basis for your investment strategy can improve the quality of your life as well.

About one year after my first book was published, I met a colleague and sophisticated investor with an M.B.A. from Wharton, University of Pennsylvania, and a B.B.A. from Wake Forest. He also had about thirty years of experience in financial management, including his last position as Assistant

Treasurer at a major corporation. After meeting with my firm, and having read my book, he was so convinced that this was the winning strategy that he wanted to help others benefit from adopting its principles. Eventually, he became a financial advisor. In short order, he completed the extensive educational requirements for his CERTIFIED FINANCIAL PLANNER(tm) certification. He later related the following story.

He told me that he used to spend many hours every day reading various financial publications, researching individual stocks and watching the financial news. And this was after spending a long and full day at the office. After learning of and adopting the principles of Modern Portfolio Theory, the Efficient Market Hypothesis and passive investing he found that he no longer needed to do those things. He recognized that he was paying attention to what was really nothing more than noise that would, at best, distract him from the winner's game.

He sat down with his wife and calculated that by adopting a passive investment approach he had actually recaptured six weeks per year of his life. It is one thing to decide to spend six weeks a year on productive activities. However, as he had now learned, not only were the activities in which he had been engaged non-productive, they actually were counterproductive because of the expenses and taxes incurred as a result of his active strategy. And, that didn't even include placing a value on the most precious resource he had: time. He recognized that time is a scarce resource. He only had a limited amount of it and did not want to spend it on less than optimal activities.

The Moral of the Tale
The moral of this tale is that indexing, and passive investing in general, not only allows you to earn market returns in a low-cost and tax efficient manner, but it also frees you from spending any time at all watching CNBC and reading financial publications that are basically not much more than what Jane Bryant Quinn called "investment pornography."

Instead, you can spend your time with your family, perform community service, read a good book or pursue your favorite hobby. Remember, investing was never meant to be exciting, despite what Wall Street and the financial media want you to believe. Investing is supposed to be about achieving your financial goals with the least amount of risk.

The next story is my own personal big rocks tale.

Chapter 24:
Don't Sweat the Small Stuff

I became the Director of Research for Buckingham Asset Management because I wanted to provide investors with the knowledge necessary to make prudent investment decisions. I wanted to help prevent the wolves of Wall Street from shearing (and in some cases slaughtering) investors as if they were sheep. Through my writings and interactions with investors I believe I have accomplished that objective—though there is a lot more work to be done.

The greatest pleasure I have received from my efforts is that many of our clients have conveyed to us the following message. "While we are pleased with the investment results, the greatest value you have added is that you have improved the quality of our lives. Armed with the knowledge of how markets really work and a well-thought-out investment plan tailored to our unique situation we are able to ignore the noise of the market and the investment pandering of Wall Street. We are now focusing on the big rocks in our lives."

In my particular case, I have been able to spend my time coaching my children's sports teams. Over the years I have coached my daughters in soccer, basketball and softball. I also have been able to attend their sporting events and dance recitals. I am also an avid reader. While I read about ten to twenty investment books a year as part of my research, I also read another fifty to sixty books annually, ranging from popular spy novels to great literature.

Indexing and passive investing have the "disadvantage" of being boring. I admit it. However, if anyone needs to get their excitement in life from investing, I suggest that they might want to consider getting another life.

Personally, my life is enriched by participating in and attending sporting events. And I get excitement from my passion, whitewater rafting. There is no question in my mind that I get all the excitement I need from life staring a Class V+ rapid in the face. I have been on over forty whitewater adventures, on over twenty different rivers, in ten different states, many of them containing Class V and Class V+ rapids. I have even experienced the thrill of going overboard on a Class V rapid on the Youghiogheny River in Maryland, and a similar thrill going down a Class V section of the Arkansas River in Colorado, which, by the way, is one thrill I can do without.

And, more importantly, I have been able to share many of those experiences with my family, especially my oldest daughter Jodi. She loves the sport so much she took canoeing classes while attending Emory University and trained to be a guide.

The Moral of the Tale

The moral of this story is that while it is a tragedy that the majority of investors unnecessarily miss out on market returns that are available to anyone by adopting a passive investment strategy, the really great tragedy in life is that they also miss out on the important things in life in pursuit of the "Holy Grail of Outperformance." My fondest wish is that this book will lead you to the winner's game in both investing and, more importantly, life.

If you find that you need excitement from your investments you should set up a special "entertainment" account. The assets inside that account should not exceed more than a few percent of your total portfolio. Then invest the rest of your assets in the winner's game.

The next story explains how to implement the winner's game in both investing and life.

We continue to make more money when snoring than when active.

—Warren Buffett

Chapter 25:
The Big Rocks Portfolio

Alan and Alice were both fifty years old and had been married for twenty years. At a dinner party the conversation turned to the subject of investing, as it does at many such parties. Several people told stories about stocks they had recently purchased. There were also tales about the big profits that had been made on a particular stock. There was also talk about the latest hot fund managers. As usual, Alan listened intently. He loved to play the market and was hoping to pick up some good tips.

The next evening over dinner the following conversation took place.

Alice: I was thinking about the conversation last night and a thought came to me. At these parties we always hear stories about the big profits our friends have made buying stocks. However, I have yet to hear a single story about any losses they have taken. Now I know our friends pretty well. If they all have been generating all those profits how come none of them are rich? Doesn't that seem strange to you?

Alan: I never thought about that.

Alice: I got up early this morning and looked over our financial records. While I know you find it fun and exciting picking stocks, our assets haven't grown as we had hoped. Looking at all the old brokerage statements, I found that you are now working with your fifth brokerage firm. It seems like none of them have done well by us. I am worried that we will not have enough saved up for retirement. I have been talking to my friend Hillary and she told me that she is working with a financial advisor with which she and Mark are happy. Not only has their portfolio done well, but Mark is now spending more time with her, instead of watching CNBC, researching stocks and talking with his broker. I think we should go talk to this advisor. In fact, I called him and we have a meeting set up for tomorrow at 10 a.m.

Alan: But Alice, I really enjoy investing and doing it myself. And by doing it myself, I feel like I am in control. I don't want some advisor telling me how to invest our money. After all, who is going to be more concerned about our assets than me.

Alice: Alan I know you enjoy it, you are concerned, and you spend a lot of time on it, but you have to admit the results have not been great. Listen to this. This morning I checked on the Internet and found that over the twenty years we have been married the market has been up 13 percent per annum. While I cannot calculate our rate of return, I don't think we have done anywhere near as well. At that rate we would have been doubling our money about every six years, and we are not even close to that.

Alan: Okay, I agree we should go talk to the advisor. It never hurts to listen.

Alice: Promise you will keep an open mind?

Alan: Sure.

The next morning they met with the advisor, Jeff Stephens. After a brief introduction and the usual pleasantries the meeting went as follows.

Jeff: It would really help me if you would tell me a bit about your investment experiences. By that I mean, any individual stocks or mutual funds you may have purchased. I would also appreciate hearing how you made those decisions. Did you use a financial advisor or stockbroker to help you make your choices, or are you a do-it-yourself investor?

It would also be great if you could tell me what thought process you used to make your decisions. For example, if you chose mutual funds, did you use Morningstar's rating system to help with that decision? Or perhaps you used the recommendations of *Money* or some other publication?

Alan: We have done a little bit of everything and have worked with a number of stockbrokers over the years. They have made recommendations, but I like to do my own research before I make a final decision. In our 401(k) plans at work we have invested in several mutual funds. Of course, I checked the past performance of the funds as well as Morningstar's rating before making the choices.

Jeff: Thanks for sharing that with me. I have just two more questions. First, can you tell me how you have done?

Alan: Okay, I guess.

Jeff: I mean specifically what rate of return have you earned over the years?

Alan: I don't know.

Jeff: Alan, let me assure you that most people I meet don't know either. However, I can tell you that all of our clients know exactly how they are doing. Every quarter they receive a statement from us showing the rate of return they have earned for that quarter, the year to date, and since they began using our services. Having that information allows both them and us to track the progress they are making toward achieving the financial objectives established in their plan. Which leads me to my second question. Do you have a written financial plan that identifies your goals and outlines how you expect to achieve them?

Alan: No. I have to admit we don't.

Jeff: Alan and Alice let me ask you this: Would you ever take a trip to a place you have never been without a road map and directions?

At this point Alice jumped in.

Alice: Alan might, but I never would. He won't even stop to ask for directions when we get lost.

Jeff: Let me also ask if you would start a business without spending lots of time and energy thoroughly researching that business and then developing a well-thought-out plan?

Alice: Of course we wouldn't.

Jeff: Nor would any other prudent businessman or woman. Investing is no different. There is an old, but wise, saying: Those that fail to plan, plan to fail. We don't think it is possible to make a rational decision about any investment without thinking about how it impacts the risk of the entire portfolio and the chances of achieving your financial goals. That is why the first thing we do after explaining our investment philosophy is to develop a plan. The plan will be one that is tailored to your circumstances. And while we will be there to help guide you, you will be the ones making the final decisions. We don't believe in cookie-cutter solutions.

Jeff went on to explain that the firm's investment philosophy was based on documented academic research, not on his own personal beliefs. He made the analogy that in the same way doctors decide on treatments based on studies published in journals such as the *New England Journal of Medicine*, the firm's investment philosophy was based on academic studies, such as those published in the *Journal of Finance*. Unfortunately, the way most individuals invest is that they get their investment advice from CNBC and *SmartMoney*. That is the medical equivalent of deciding on a treatment based on advice from *People* or the *Ladies Home Journal*.

Jeff explained that in simple terms the strategy was based on the belief that trying to pick stocks and time the market was really a loser's game. While Alan and Alice might know someone who has outperformed the market, it is likely that the majority of the people they know have not done so. Then, he showed them the academic evidence to support his statements and discussed how they could achieve great returns without trying to beat the market. And certainly by not trying to beat the market they were likely to outperform most of their friends as well as the majority of professional investors.

Alice turned to Alan and said, "Now wouldn't that be a great story to tell at one of those cocktail parties."

Jeff went on to explain that since trying to beat the market was a loser's game, the winning strategy was to build a globally diversified portfolio and then basically be a buy-and-hold investor. Diversification prevented clients from having too many eggs in one basket. And buy-and-hold accomplished several objectives.

First, it meant low costs because funds that don't try to pick stocks or time the market don't have to employ expensive managers. Second, buying and holding keeps trading costs down, costs which are likely to reduce returns. Third, minimizing trading results in high tax efficiency—they would not be sharing as much of their gains with Uncle Sam. And finally, and perhaps most importantly, Alan could stop spending time trying to beat the market. That would allow him to spend more time with Alice and their children. Jeff then went on to tell them the story of the "Big Rocks."

After completing the story of the Big Rocks, Jeff showed Alan and Alice the following table. He called it the Big Rocks portfolios. He noted that the Big Rocks portfolios were really samples of the type of portfolios his firm built for clients. He made clear that because each client had a unique situation, the Big Rocks portfolios he was showing them were just models, or starting points for discussions. Jeff also made clear that while Alan's and Alice's portfolio would likely end up looking similar to those in the table, it might also be somewhat different.

Big Rocks Portfolios–Asset Allocations

	Conservative	Moderate	Moderately Agressive	Highly Agressive
Equity (%)	**40**	**60**	**80**	**100**
US Stocks (%)	**28**	**42**	**56**	**70**
Large (%)	6	9	12	15
Large Value (%)	6	9	12	15
Small (%)	6	9	12	15
Small Value (%)	6	9	12	15
Real Estate (%)	4	6	8	10
International Stocks (%)	**12**	**18**	**24**	**30**
Large (%)	2	3	4	5
Large Value (%)	4	6	8	10
Small (%)	2	3	4	5
Small Value (%)	2	3	4	5
Emerging Markets (%)	2	3	4	5
Fixed Income (%)	**60**	**40**	**20**	**0**
Short-Term Bonds (%)	60	40	20	0

Jeff explained that each of the left hand columns represented a mutual fund that in simple terms bought-and-held hundreds, if not thousands, of different stocks—the majority of stocks in that asset class. He explained that an asset class was simply a group of securities that had similar risk characteris-

161

tics. There are large stocks and small stocks, value and growth stocks, real estate and domestic and international stocks. And there are also risky equities and safer fixed income investments. Jeff noted that by controlling the amount of assets in each asset class, Alan and Alice would be in total control of the risks they were taking. Jeff also noted that every Big Rocks portfolio was well diversified with investments in many asset classes. This would avoid the problem of having too many eggs in one basket.

After reviewing the table, Jeff showed them the kind of returns that could have been earned by investors had they adopted one of the Big Rocks portfolios. Alice was surprised to see that despite taking less risk even the conservative portfolio had produced better results than they had been able to achieve.

When discussing the returns of the various Big Rocks portfolios, Jeff was careful to point out that while the highly aggressive portfolio had produced the highest returns, that fact didn't necessarily make it the best choice. The greater returns were a reflection of the greater risk involved. Finally, Jeff made clear that the returns they were looking at were the result of historical evidence and that the future might look very different. The only thing that could be controlled was the amount of risk they would be taking. They could not control the outcome. Having said that, the Big Rocks strategy would give them the best chance to achieve their goals while taking only the amount of risk that was appropriate to their situation.

Jeff then explained that if Alan and Alice decided to become clients the next step would be to set up another meeting. The goal of that meeting would be to first determine their financial goals and then determine if those goals were realistic. If they were realistic, the next step would be to determine if they were willing and able to take the risk needed to achieve them. If they were not, he would work with them to help determine whether their goals or current lifestyle would need to be adjusted.

Once that process was completed, he would help them design a written plan in the form of an investment policy statement that Alan and Alice would sign. This would evidence their commitment to the plan.

Everything she heard appealed to Alice. She felt that it was exactly what she was looking for. She told Jeff that she had a question for him.

Alice: Jeff, this all sounds great. Can you explain to us how you get paid?

Jeff: I am glad you asked. We are a fee-only advisor. Our fee is based on a percentage of the assets you ask us to advise you on. We do not accept commissions, or any other form of compensation, from anyone. The only compensation we receive is from you and the only thing we sell is our advice. This helps us avoid conflicts of interest, allowing us to be on the same side of the table as are our clients. Unlike stockbrokers, who make money if you trade or by selling proprietary products that earn fees for their firm, we make money by helping you do well.

That clinched the deal for Alice.

Alice: Jeff, I think I can speak for both of us. I want to thank you for taking the time to explain your firm's philosophy and how you work with investors. We would like to become clients.

Jeff: I am pleased to hear that. However, I need to explain that we do not accept all investors as clients. We will only agree to work with those investors who fully understand our approach and are willing to commit to adhering to their well-thought-out plan for a very long time. We fully expect that you would fire us if we fail to provide the kind of *service* and *investment advice* that we have agreed upon. Those are things we can control. The *returns* your portfolio will actually generate, however, are determined by things beyond anyone's control. All we can control are the risks taken, and that is determined by your asset allocation. If you are going to determine the success of the strategy by short-term results, we are the wrong firm for you.

What I would like you to do is to take this book, *Rational Investing in Irrational Times*, and read it carefully. It is a gift. If you enjoy it, pass it on to a friend you think might benefit from reading it. The book explains the mistakes that even smart investors make, why they make them and how to avoid them. In effect, it explains our investment philosophy and addresses many of the issues we have discussed. It is an easy read too. After reading the book, give us a call and let us know if you are convinced that this is the right strategy for you, and if you are willing to commit to it for the long term. If the answer is yes, as I hope it will be, then we will do everything in our power to demonstrate that we deserve the trust you will have placed in us.

And one more thing. Alan, I noted that you do enjoy picking stocks. While we don't recommend it, we would be willing to set up an "entertainment account" for you. You can trade all you want in that account. And while we won't charge you for an account we are not advising you on, we will report to you the returns on that account. In that way you will be able to see for the first time how you are actually doing.

Alan: That sounds good.

Alice: Thank you for the time and the book. While I don't normally read books on investing, I promise that we will *both* read this one and get back to you in a couple of weeks.

Two weeks later Alice called Jeff. She told him that Alan actually found himself laughing as he recognized that he had made many of the mistakes discussed in the book. Now Alice and Alan understood why they had not achieved the kind of returns that they should have earned given the risks they had taken. In fact, Alan had given up the idea of an entertainment account. He decided that there were other hobbies that were just as much fun, but a lot less expensive. And they lived happily ever after.

The Moral of the Tale

The moral of this tale is that just because you enjoy doing something, doesn't mean that you are good at it. Nor does it mean that the time you spend on the endeavor is the most productive use of that time.

The next tale explains why investors who have implemented the types of passive strategies recommended in this book have experienced "the best of times." On the other hand, for those that continue to play the game of active investing, in general, it has been "the worst of times."

Wall Street doesn't have to keep confessing its sins. It just has to stop committing them.

—James Surowiecki, "The Talking Cure," *New Yorker*, December 9, 2002

Chapter 26:
A Tale of Two Strategies

"It was the best of times, it was the worst of times." These are among the most famous words in all of literature. They are the opening lines of *A Tale of Two Cities*, Charles Dickens's tale of the French Revolution. However, those words apply just as well today to the world of investing.

For many investors, the first years of the twenty-first century have been the worst of times. The mutual fund industry has been plagued by a series of scandals highlighting the many conflicts of interest that exist in much (but certainly not all) of that world.

In addition, despite the obvious economies of scale and the tremendous growth of assets under management, mutual fund fees are now, on average, higher than ever. And, unfortunately, investors have learned that paying high fees for actively managed mutual funds has proven to be a losing strategy—even when the funds have had excellent track records.

The bottom line is that over the long term the majority of actively managed funds underperform an appropriate passive benchmark. The performance comparison only becomes worse when after-tax returns are the measure. And no one has demonstrated the ability to persistently identify the few future winners ahead of time.

This is what Morningstar, a company that makes most of its money selling performance data and its mutual fund rating service, had to say about expenses and performance. "Expense ratios are the best predictors of performance—way better than historical returns. It's tempting to look at strong past performance and assume a fund can repeat its success, but there's no guarantee it will. In fact, we've found that you'd be better off randomly picking a fund with expenses in the cheapest quartile and past returns in the worst quartile than a fund with returns in the top quartile and expenses in the highest quartile. Higher expenses don't get you better management. If it did you'd expect higher-cost funds to outperform their lower-cost peers—when in fact just the opposite has happened."[1]

On the other hand, for investors who believe that markets are efficient and that passive investing is the winning strategy, it has been the best of times. There has been a dramatic increase in the availability of passively managed funds—index funds, exchange traded funds (ETFs), and passive asset class funds. More fund choices are available in more asset classes (e.g., real estate, emerging markets, commodities, TIPS) allowing investors to more effectively diversify their portfolios. In addition, while passively managed funds are almost by definition relatively more tax efficient than actively managed funds (because of their relatively low turnover), several fund families have introduced passively managed funds that are also tax-managed as well, further improving after-tax returns. And the good news does not end there.

While actively managed funds have been delivering on average poor performance and raising fees, passively managed funds have been delivering market returns at already low costs and yet lowering fees. Both Fidelity and Vanguard have lowered fees on many of their index funds and ETFs. And Dimensional Fund Advisors, the leading provider of passive asset class funds, also continues to lower fees. These fund families are actually delivering on the promise of economies of scale.

The Moral of the Tale
When Dickens wrote those famous opening words perhaps he knew that they would be applicable to all times. They certainly are applicable to investors today. For the majority of those that continue to place their faith in the practice of active management, it has been the "age of foolishness, the season of Darkness, and the winter of despair." On the other hand, for those that have adopted a passive investment strategy it has been "the age of wisdom, the season of Light and the spring of hope." And that is the moral of this tale.

The next tale provides guidance to those investors who believe they are best served by working with a financial advisor. It provides the road map to help you identify one you can trust.

Chapter 27:
How to Identify an Advisor
You Can Trust

When it comes to home repairs individuals can be categorized into two broad groups. The first group is what we might call the "Home Depot Crowd," the do-it-yourselfers (DIY). This group has many subgroups. One subgroup belongs because they believe they can do it cheaper than the cost of hiring a professional. Another belongs because they like the work, have the skills to do the work well and enjoy seeing the fruits of their labor.

Some of the individuals who belong to the DIY group should not be there. These individuals belong because they are trying to save money (though they might even enjoy doing the work), but, unfortunately, they don't have the skills required to be sure that the job will be well done. And if something is not done right the first time, the cost of correcting errors can far exceed what it would have cost to pay a professional to do it right in the first place. Those people who belong to the second group should follow what I call the Swedroe Principle: *If something is worth doing, it is worth paying someone to do it for you.* It might be that you follow that principle because you place a high value on your free time and can afford to pay to have the work done. It might also be that you don't enjoy doing the work. And, if you are like me, you belong because if there is a way to screw it up you will find it.

When it comes to investing there are also those same two groups. Within the DIY group you have the same types of subgroups. You have those that belong because they don't want to pay a professional for something they believe they can do just as well. Unfortunately, the evidence from academic studies demonstrates that there are few individuals with the investment knowledge and discipline to be successful investors. Had those studies compared the two skills, it is likely that they would have found that DIYers who attempt to perform home repairs fare better than their DIY investor counterparts. And the costs of making bad investment decisions almost certainly exceeds the costs of repairing that leaky faucet.

There are also individuals that recognize that they have neither the knowledge nor the discipline required to be successful on their own. They also recognize that a good financial advisor can add value in many ways. There are also individuals that would rather have someone else focus on financial matters so that they can focus more of their attention on the more important things in their lives, their "Big Rocks." They know that even if they had the skills to do it themselves, the time spent on financial matters is time not spent with family, friends, doing community service, etc. And they place a greater value on that time than on the cost of an advisor.

For those who wish to go it alone, this book has provided you not only with the winning strategy of global diversification and passive investing but also the Big Rocks portfolios—providing guidance on constructing a portfolio that meets your unique ability, willingness and need to take risk. And the Appendix provides a list of recommended investment vehicles to use. For those that recognize the value of a good financial advisor the following advice is offered.

One of the most important decisions an investor can make is the choice of a financial advisor. When making this selection, surveys show that along with the financial expertise of the advisor, investors look for someone they can trust. However, trust is an intangible quality that cannot be as easily quantified as, for example, a baseball player's batting average. Thus, when interviewing a potential financial advisor, require them to make the following eleven commitments to you. Doing so will give you the greatest chance of avoiding conflicts of interest and the greatest chance of achieving your financial goals.

1. The firm should be able to demonstrate that its guiding principle is to provide investment advisor services that are in the client's best interests.

2. The firm follows a fiduciary standard of care—a fiduciary standard is often considered the highest legal duty that one party can have to another. This differs from the suitability standard present in many brokerage firms. That standard only requires that a product or service be suitable—it does not have to be in the investor's best interest.

3. The firm serves as a fee-only advisor—avoiding the conflicts that commission-based compensation can create. With commission-based compensation, it can be difficult to know if the investment or product recommended by the advisor is the one that is best for you, or the one that generates greater compensation for the advisor.

4. All potential conflicts are fully disclosed.

5. Advice is based on the latest academic research, not on opinions.

6. The firm is client centric—advisors focus on delivering sound advice and targeted solutions. The only requirement they have in offering

172

particular solutions is whether the client's best interests will be served.

7. Advisors deliver a high level of personal attention and develop strong personal relationships—and clients benefit from a team of professionals to help them make sound financial decisions.
8. Advisors invest their personal assets (including the firm's profit-sharing plan) based on the same set of investment principles and in the same or comparable securities that they recommend to their clients.
9. They develop investment plans that are integrated with estate, tax and risk management (insurance) plans. The overall plans are tailored to each client's unique personal situation.
10. Their advice is goal-oriented—evaluating each decision not in isolation, but in terms of its impact on the likelihood of success of the overall plan.
11. Comprehensive wealth management services are provided by individuals that have the CFP, PFS, or other comparable designations.

The Moral of the Tale

There are certainly some individuals that have the knowledge, time, interest, and discipline to develop a well-thought-out investment plan. But that is only the necessary condition for success. The sufficient condition is to also be able to integrate the investment plan with a carefully planned estate, tax and risk management plan. They also have to be able to manage the plan (rebalance and tax loss harvest) on an ongoing basis in a cost and tax efficient manner. And that is not all. They must also be able to adapt the plan to meet changing circumstances and the passage of time. Unfortunately, the evidence is that fewer people have those skills than believe they have them. As we have discussed, overconfidence is a common human trait.

Fortunately, for those that recognize that they would be best served by hiring a professional advisor, good advice doesn't have to be expensive. However, bad, or untrustworthy, advice almost always will cost you dearly, no matter how little you pay for it. Therefore, you should perform a thorough due diligence before choosing a financial advisor. That due diligence should not only include requesting the advisor make the aforementioned eleven commitments to you, but it should also include a careful review of form ADV—a disclosure document setting forth information about the advisor, including the investment strategy, fee schedules, conflicts of interest, regulatory incidents and so on. Careful due diligence will minimize the risk of having to make expensive repairs.

Conclusion

One of my favorite films is *The Man Who Shot Liberty Valance*. The film is a western about a greenhorn, pacifist lawyer (Jimmy Stewart) who stands up to and then shoots and kills the villain, Liberty Valance (Lee Marvin). The story is told using the device of a flashback. Stewart, a U.S. senator, returns to his hometown to attend the funeral of his best friend (John Wayne). In an interview with a young newspaper reporter, Stewart finally tells the true story of the legendary gunfight. The reporter learns that it was not Stewart who actually killed Liberty Valance. Instead, it was John Wayne. Excited about his great discovery, the reporter races off to his editor. When the editor finishes reading this incredible tale, he rips the reporter's notes to shreds and tells him: "When the legend becomes fact, print the legend."

Wall Street and the financial media need and want to keep alive the myth that active investing is the winning strategy. Thus, they fight extremely hard to keep the legends and myths about active investing alive. The goal of this book was to kill the legends by exposing them as myths. The introduction set forth three objectives to achieve that goal.

- Demonstrate through the use of stories and analogies how markets *really* work, exposing many investment legends as nothing more than investment propaganda.
- Change the way you think about investing and how markets work.
- Provide you with sufficient knowledge to begin to make informed and prudent investment decisions—in other words, to stop throwing your hard earned money away.

Hopefully, the book has been successful in meeting those objectives. If it has, your next step should be to develop a well-thought-out financial plan that identifies your unique ability, willingness and need to take risk. The financial plan should also be integrated with an estate, tax and risk management (insurance) plan. And the plan should include an asset allocation table, like the one in the tale, The Big Rocks Portfolio.

When designing *your* Big Rocks portfolio it is critical that you remember that we live in a world of uncertainty. Despite what Wall Street and the media would like you to believe, there are no clear crystal balls, only cloudy ones. And in a world of uncertainty, the best defense is broad global diversification across many different asset classes. For the equity allocation of your portfolio that means including some exposure to domestic and international stocks

175

(including emerging markets), small-cap and large-cap stocks, value and growth stocks and real estate. Investors should also consider including some exposure to commodities (though only in the form of a passive investment vehicle).

After writing your plan, it is also important that you sign it, demonstrating your commitment to the plan. Having done so you should implement the plan by purchasing passively managed funds—index funds (including ETFs) or passive asset class funds. Then, unless an underlying assumption of your plan has changed, the only actions you should be taking are to regularly rebalance the portfolio to the allocation targets you established and to tax loss harvest whenever the opportunity arises. Fortunately, these should be easy things to do. The hard part for most investors is ignoring the noise of the market, the Wall Street Establishment, the media and the emotions caused by all the noise. Unfortunately, emotions, like greed and envy in bull markets and fear and panic in bear markets, have often caused even the best laid out plans to end up in the trash heap.

Thus, one last bit of advice is offered: Cancel all subscriptions to mass media investment publications and newsletters, turn off CNBC, and, finally, focus on the BIG ROCKS in your life. By doing so, you are likely to have not only a richer portfolio, but a richer life as well. That is why passive investing is the winner's game in life as well as investing.

In closing, one of the great pleasures for me has been hearing from so many readers of my five prior books. So if you have any questions, or if you would like to discuss any of the concepts covered in this book, feel free to e-mail me at lswedroe@bamstl.com.

Appendix A:
The Big Rocks Portfolio
Investment Vehicle Recommendations

The following is a list of funds recommended for use as the building blocks for a Big Rocks portfolio. While the Big Rocks Portfolios table did not include an allocation to commodities, you should at least consider a small allocation to this asset class (reducing the equity allocation accordingly). To benefit from the risk reduction properties that commodities can offer (if the right vehicle is used), an allocation of from 3 to 5 percent up to as much as 10 percent is recommended. The more risk averse the investor, and the more they are exposed to the risk of inflation, the higher should be the allocation to this asset class. For a full discussion on why commodities are recommended see Appendix H of *The Only Guide to a Winning Investment Strategy You'll Ever Need* (2005 edition).

Note that funds with an asterisk are tax managed (TM) and, therefore, are strongly recommended for taxable accounts. Two asterisks mean that the fund is appropriate for only tax-advantaged accounts (e.g., IRAs, 401(k)s, 403(b)s, profit sharing plans or non-taxable accounts, such as those of pension plans or non-profit organizations).

Domestic Equities

Large Cap
Bridgeway Blue-Chip 35*
DFA Large Company
DFA TM U.S. Equity*
Dreyfus Basic S&P 500 Stock Index
Fidelity Spartan 500 Index
SSgA S&P 500 Index
USAA S&P 500 Index
Vanguard 500 Index
DFA Enhanced U.S. Large**
iShares S&P 500 Index
Fidelity Spartan Total Market Index
Vanguard Total Stock Market Index
Vanguard Total Stock Market ETF
iShares Russell 1000 Index
iShares Russell 3000 Index
iShares Dow Jones Total Market Index

International Equities

Large Cap
DFA Large Cap International
Fidelity Spartan International Index
Vanguard Developed Markets Index
Vanguard European Stock Index
Vanguard Pacific Stock Index
Vanguard TM International*
Vanguard Total International Stock Index
iShares MSCI EAFE Index
iShares S&P Europe 350 Index
iShares S&P TOPIX 150 Index (Japan)
iShares MSCI Pacific ex-Japan Index

Large-Cap Value
DFA U.S. Large Cap Value
DFA TM U.S. Marketwide Value*
Vanguard Value Index
iShares Russell 1000 Value Index

Large-Cap Value
DFA International Value
DFA TM International Value*
iShares EAFE Value Index

Small Cap
Bridgeway Ultra-Small Company Market
DFA U.S. Small Cap
DFA TM U.S. Small Cap*
DFA Micro Cap
Vanguard Small Cap Index
Vanguard TM Small Cap*
iShares S&P Small Cap 600 Index
iShares Russell Microcap Index

Small Cap
DFA International Small Company

Small-Cap Value
DFA U.S. Small Cap Value
DFA TM U.S. Targeted Value*
Vanguard Small Cap Value Index
iShares S&P 600 Value

Small-Cap Value
DFA International Small Cap Value

Real Estate**
DFA Real Estate Securities
Vanguard REIT Index
iShares Cohen & Steers Realty Majors Index
iShares Dow Jones Real Estate Index

Emerging Markets
DFA Emerging Markets
DFA Emerging Markets Small Cap
DFA Emerging Markets Value
DFA Emerging Markets Core
Vanguard Emerging Markets Index
iShares Emerging Markets Index

Commodities
PIMCO Commodity Real Return**
iPath Dow Jones-AIG Commodity Index Total Return ETN

Fixed Income: Taxable
DFA 1-Year Global
DFA 2-Year Global
DFA 5-Year Global
DFA 5-Year Government
DFA Intermediate Government

Fixed Income: Tax-Exempt
DFA Short-Term Municipal Bond Portfolio
Vanguard Short-Term Tax-Free
Vanguard Limited-Term Tax-Free
Vanguard Intermediate Term Tax-Free

iShares 1–3 Year Treasury Index
iShares 7–10 Year Treasury Index
TIAA-CREF Fixed Income Annuities
Vanguard Short-Term Treasury
Vanguard Short-Term Federal
Vanguard Short-Term Bond Index
Vanguard Intermediate-Term Index
Vanguard Inflation-Protected Securities**
iShares TIPS**
I bonds

Investors need to be aware that the DFA funds are only available through approved financial advisors. There are several hundred such advisors around the country.

Notes

Chapter 2. How Markets Set Prices
1. William J. Bernstein, *The Four Pillars of Investing* (McGraw-Hill, 2002), p. 297.
2. Raymond D. Sauer, "The Economics of Wagering Markets," *Journal of Economic Literature*, 36, p. 2021-64.
3. James Surowiecki, *The Wisdom of Crowds* (Doubleday, 2004), p. 13-14.
4. Edited by Peter Bernstein and Aswath Damodaran, *Investment Management*, p. 15.
5. Brad Barber and Terrance Odean, "Trading Is Hazardous to Your Wealth: The Common Stock Investment Performance of Individual Investors," *Journal of Finance* (April 2000).
6. Brad Barber and Terrance Odean, "Boys Will Be Boys: Gender, Overconfidence and Common Stock Investment," *Quarterly Journal of Economics* (February 2001).
7. Brad Barber and Terrance Odean, "Trading Is Hazardous to Your Wealth."
8. Brad Barber and Terrance Odean, "Too Many Cooks Spoil the Profits: Investment Club Performance," *Financial Analysts Journal* (January/February 2000).
9. Andrew Tobias, *The Only Investment Book You Will Ever Need* (Harcourt, 1978).
10. Mark M. Carhart, "On Persistence in Mutual Fund Performance," Doctoral Dissertation, University of Chicago, December 1994.
11. James Surowiecki, *The Wisdom of Crowds* (Doubleday, 2004), p. 51.
12. William Berlind, "Bookies in Exile," *New York Times*, August 17, 2003.

Chapter 3. The Twenty-Dollar Bill
1. Dwight Lee and James Verbrugge, "The Efficient Market Theory Thrives on Criticism," *Journal of Applied Corporate Finance*, (Spring 1996).
2. Burton G. Malkiel, "Are Markets Efficient? Yes, Even If They Make Errors," *Wall Street Journal*, December 28, 2000.

Chapter 4. Persistence of Performance
1. Dr. Mark Rubinstein, "Rational Markets: Yes or No? The Affirmative Case," *Financial Analysts Journal* (May-June 2001).
2. Ron Ross, *The Unbeatable Market* (Optimum Press, 2002), p. 57.
3. Dr. Mark Rubinstein.

4. Raymond Fazzi, "Going Their Own Way," *Financial Advisor* (March 2001).
5. Ralph Wanger, *A Zebra in Lion Country* (Simon & Schuster, 1997).
6. Peter Bernstein, *Against the Gods* (Wiley, 1996).

Chapter 5. The Demon of Chance
1. Karen Damato and Allison Bisbey Colter, "Hedge Funds, Once Utterly Exclusive, Lure Less-Elite Investors," *Wall Street Journal*, January 3, 2002.
2. Jonathan Clements, *25 Myths You've Got to Avoid* (Simon & Schuster, 1998), p. 86.

Chapter 6. When Even the Best Aren't Likely to Win
1. John Bogle, "The Stock Market Universe—Stars, Comets, and the Sun," speech before the Financial Analysts of Philadelphia, February 15, 2001.
2. Mark Hulbert, "A Realignment of the Stars in the Mutual Fund Sky," *New York Times*, May 19, 2002.
3. David Rynecki, "Stargazers Beware," *Fortune* (July 8, 2002).
4. FutureMetrics and Dimensional Fund Advisors.
5. Philip Halpern, Nancy Calkins and Tom Ruggels, "Does the Emperor Wear Clothes or Not?" *Financial Analysts Journal* (July/August 1996).
6. "Hard Wired," *Dow Jones Asset Management* (November/December 1998).

Chapter 7. Outfoxing the Box
1. Robert D. Arnott, Andrew L. Berkin, and Jia Ye, "How Well Have Taxable Investors Been Served in the 1980s and 1990s?" *Journal of Portfolio Management* (Summer 2000).
2. Charles Ellis, *Investment Policy: How to Win the Loser's Game* (Irwin, 1993) p. 24.

Chapter 11. Buy What You Know
1. Gur Huberman, "Familiarity Breeds Investment," Working Paper (November 1999).
2. Kenneth R. French and James M. Poterba, "Investor Diversification and International Equity Markets," *American Economic Review*, vol. 81, no. 2, 222–26.

Chapter 12. Why Did I Buy That Stock?

1. Greg Ip, "Stocks That Are Covered by Few Analysts Have Stronger Rallies on Profit Surprises," *Wall Street Journal*, July 14, 1997.
2. Peter Bernstein, *Against the Gods* (Wiley, 1996).
3. Brad Barber and Terrance Odean, "Too Many Cooks Spoil the Profits: Investment Club Performance," *Financial Analysts Journal* (January/February 2000).

Chapter 14. Too Many Eggs in One Basket
1. Ron Ross, *The Unbeatable Market* (Optimum Press, 2002), p. 157.

Chapter 15. Confusing Before-the-Fact Strategy and After-the-Fact Outcome
1. Michael J. Mauboussin, *More Than You Know*, (Columbia University Press, 2006), p. 10.
2. Nassim Nicholas Taleb, *Fooled by Randomness* (Texere, 2001).

Chapter 16. An Investor's Worst Enemy
1. Jonathan Fuerbringer, "Investing It," *New York Times*, March 30, 1997.
2. Robert McGough, "The Secret (Active) Dreams of an Indexer," *Wall Street Journal*, February 25, 1997.
3. Peter Bernstein, *The Portable MBA in Investment* (Wiley, 1995).
4. Jonathan Clements, *25 Myths You've Got to Avoid* (Simon & Schuster, 1998), p. 55.
5. James H. Smalhout, "Too Close to Your Money?" *Bloomberg Personal* (November 1997).
6. Gary Belsky and Thomas Gilovich, *Why Smart People Make Big Money Mistakes* (Simon & Schuster, 1999).
7. Peter L. Bernstein and Aswath Damodaran (editors), *Investment Management* (Wiley, 1998), p. 252.
8. Ron Ross, *The Unbeatable Market* (Optimum Press, 2002), p. 16.
9. Jonathan Clements, "Getting Going: Twenty Tips for No-Nonsense Investing," *Wall Street Journal*, February 19, 2006.

Chapter 17. A Higher Intelligence
1. W. Scott Simon, *The Prudent Investor Act* (Namborn Publishing, 2002) p. 125.

Chapter 18. Even With a Clear Crystal Ball
1. William Sherden, *The Fortune Sellers* (Wiley, 1998).

Chapter 19. Be Careful What You Ask For
1. Encyclopedia Mythica.
2. Jim Davis, "Economic Growth and Emerging Market Returns," August 2006.

Chapter 22. Mad Money
1. Michael Learmonth, "Ratings Flood for Fox, CNN," *Variety*, September 27, 2005.
2. Joseph Engelberg, Caroline Sasseville and Jared Williams, "Is the Market Mad? Evidence from *Mad Money*," Working Paper, Kellogg School of Management, Northwestern University, March 22, 2006.
3. Ibid.
4. Virginia Baldwin Hick, "Defying Physics Experts: Economy Will Keep on Rolling," *St. Louis Post-Dispatch*, October 4, 1997.

Chapter 23. The Big Rocks
1. Paul Samuelson, Quoted in Jonathan Burton, *Investment Titans* (McGraw-Hill, 2001).

Chapter 26. A Tale of Two Strategies
1. Russel Kinnel, "Expenses Trend Down, but Total Fees Keep Rising," *Morningstar Fund Investor* (April 2005).

Acknowledgments

No book is ever the work of one individual. This book is certainly no exception. I thank my partners at Buckingham Asset Management and BAM Advisor Services, Susan Shackelford-Davis, Paul Forman, Steve Funk, Bob Gellman, Ed Goldberg, Joe Hempen, Ken Katzif, Mont Levy, Steve Lourie, Vladimir Masek, Bert Schweizer III, and Stuart Zimmerman for their support, encouragement, and the freedom and time to write. And RC Balaban and Steve Nothum were a great help with the fact checking and data. I also thank Weston Wellington of Dimensional Fund Advisors for *dredging up* the hypothetical fund example.

A special word of thanks goes to Laura Latragna who not only did a great job with editing suggestions, but she helped create the tale *A Higher Intelligence*.

I want to also thank Jim Wiandt for his enthusiastic support of this book, making its publication possible.

My appreciation is expressed to my agent, Sam Fleishman, for encouraging me to write this book. I cannot imagine a better relationship between author and agent.

The most important contributions were made by the love of my life, my wife Mona. No matter the hour, she patiently read through numerous drafts and made many valuable suggestions. If the stories and analogies help make difficult concepts easy to understand, she deserves much of the credit. Words alone cannot expression my appreciation for her support and understanding for the lost weekends and the many nights that I sat at the computer well into the early morning hours. She has always provided whatever support was needed, and then some. Without that support this book would not have been possible. Walking through life with her has truly been a gracious experience.

Index

A

academic research, 105, 123, 125, 146, 159, 171–72
Aces Gold Casino, 28–29
active investing
    See also costs
    efficient markets and, 23, 28, 31–34, 117–19, 141–42
    market timing, 7, 27–28, 125–28, 145–47
    passive investing vs., 49–55, 57–59, 111–15, 117–19, 149–51
    performance, 27, 49–55, 167–68
    picking individual stocks, 7, 27–28, 113–15, 145–47
advisors. See brokers; financial advisors
Against the Gods (Bernstein), 39–40
aging population, 91–94
Allen, Woody, 18
American Law Institute, 117–18
analyst recommendations, 85–88, 145–47
Army *vs.* Duke analogy, 17–29
asset allocation, 11, 73–77, 161–63, 175–76
astronomy and astrology, 135
athletes and investment managers compared, 37–40
AT&T, 81

B

Baby Bells, 81
Bachelier, Louis, 87
Baker, David, 46
Barber, Brad, 27
baseball analogy, 37–40
basketball analogies, 17–29, 141–42
Beardstown Ladies investment club, 88
Belsky, Gary, 81, 114
Bernstein, Bill, 19
Bernstein, Peter, 39–40, 114
betting on sporting events, 17–29

D

E

F

G

H

I

J

JC Penney, 24–26, 68–69
Johnson, Randy, 38
Journal of Portfolio Management (Bernstein), 39–40

K

Kahneman, Daniel, 54–55
Kepler, Johannes, 135
knowledge vs. information, 79–82, 85–88, 93–94
Kodak, 81
Krzyzewski, Mike, 17

L

large-cap stocks, 45–46, 66–67, 74–75, 124, 139, 140–41
Larry Swedroe Investment Fund, 43–44
Lee, Dwight, 32
legal approach to investing, 117–19
Legg Mason Value Trust, 45–47
Lindner Large-Cap Fund, 45–46
luck *vs.* skill, 43–47, 109, 139–43
Lynch, Peter, 46, 81

M

Maddux, Greg, 38
"Mad Money" (CNBC), 145–47
male investor performance, 27
The Man Who Shot Liberty Valance (film), 175
market-impact costs, 23, 141
markets
    See also pricing
    efficient, 20–23, 28, 31–34, 117–19, 141–42
    forecasting, 123–25, 128, 131–33, 135–37
    spread and, 18–26, 39, 69, 141
market timing, 7, 27–28, 125–28, 145–47
MCI, 100
media
    financial incentives of, 53–54, 175
    knowledge *vs.* information, 87–88
    "Mad Money," 145–47

"outfoxing the box" game, 57–59

prudent investment strategy, 117–19

Q

R

S